高校英语选修课系列教材

READING CHINA IN ENGLISH

读懂中国
英语读写教程

主编：王 革
编者：李中正 伍怡然 吴于勤
　　　夏 芬 王丽虹

清華大学出版社
北京

内 容 简 介

本书共设8个单元,分别围绕教育全球化、跨文化交流、中国生态、中国美食、中国教育、中国家庭、中国电影、中国网红等主题展开。每单元精选3篇文章,以单元主题为主线,让学生通过阅读思辨、书面表达和项目实施等多样化练习,培养其中国题材英语材料的翻译能力和中国元素的英语表达能力。附录部分还提供了练习答案、各单元Text A和Text B的参考译文。本书附配PPT课件以及教学大纲,可登录ftp:// ftp.tup.tsinghua.edu.cn/ 下载。

本书可作为非外语专业的全校通识课及公共英语选修课、外语专业的"思政课"、来华留学生的"中国文化课"教材,也可供国际传媒和英语爱好者阅读参考。

版权所有,侵权必究。举报:010-62782989,beiqinquan@tup.tsinghua.edu.cn。

图书在版编目(CIP)数据

读懂中国:英语读写教程/王革主编.—北京:清华大学出版社,2021.8
高校英语选修课系列教材
ISBN 978-7-302-58324-0

Ⅰ. ①读… Ⅱ. ①王… Ⅲ. ①英语—阅读教学—高等学校—教材 ②英语—写作—高等学校—教材
Ⅳ. ① H319.39

中国版本图书馆CIP数据核字(2021)第109245号

责任编辑:倪雅莉
封面设计:子 一
责任校对:王凤芝
责任印制:刘海龙

出版发行:清华大学出版社
　　　网　　址:http://www.tup.com.cn, http://www.wqbook.com
　　　地　　址:北京清华大学学研大厦A座　邮　编:100084
　　　社 总 机:010-62770175　　邮　购:010-62786544
　　　投稿与读者服务:010-62776969, c-service@tup.tsinghua.edu.cn
　　　质量反馈:010-62772015, zhiliang@tup.tsinghua.edu.cn
印 装 者:小森印刷霸州有限公司
经　　销:全国新华书店
开　　本:185mm×260mm　　印　张:10.75　　字　数:226千字
版　　次:2021年8月第1版　　　　　　　印　次:2021年8月第1次印刷
定　　价:52.00元

产品编号:091889-01

讲好中国故事

Foreword 序

讲好中国故事，首先要有"好故事"。中国有数千年不间断的历史、文化，有悠久且充满活力的语言文字。文献汗牛充栋，故事耳不暇听。从中遴选出"好故事"，需要眼光，需下功夫。故事是讲给他人听的，不仅自己觉得好，更要听者觉得好，因此需要做到以下几点：一要听得懂，二要喜欢听，三要有所获。

细究起来，"讲好故事"在语法上是个歧义结构，可以分析为：A、讲/好故事；B 讲好/故事。A 中的"好"是"故事"的定语，B 中的"好"是"讲"的补语。这个歧义结构正好表明两层意思，即讲故事不仅要有"好故事"，还要把故事"讲好"。把故事讲好，首要是尊重听者，平等对待听者，包容不同文化的听者；其次要选好语种，善于运用多种媒体；同时还要有讲故事的高超技巧。

我年轻时，电影电视还不普及，说书人、戏班子在农村最受欢迎。一夜一夜跟着说书人听故事，一个集镇一个集镇跟着戏班子看戏。听了故事看了戏，自己还会讲给别人听。许多情节至今还能记得，故事中、戏文中宣扬的"礼义廉耻""忠孝节义"等精神，也成为自己思想的一部分。他们的故事成了"我的故事"。讲好中国故事的最高境界，也应是这些故事能够成为"听者的故事"，他们听了能吸收，听了能去讲。

每个民族都有自己的"好故事"。这些故事所包含的理想甚至都很近似,比如"小康""大同"的思想、建立人类命运共同体的愿望等。中国的故事不仅是中国的,也是世界的。在讲中国故事的同时,也要乐意倾听他人的故事。他人的故事,也是人类命运共同体的故事。

王革教授主编的《读懂中国:英语读写教程》,是一本让学生用英文"读懂中国"的书,也是一本教学生用英文"讲好中国故事"的书。书中素材选自《中国日报》、《环球时报》、人民网,英国的《金融时报》、《卫报》、《经济学人》、BBC,美国的《纽约时报》等英文媒体,体裁包括新闻、评论、书信、随笔、传记等,充分反映了改革开放40多年来中国在政治、经济、文化和社会生活方方面面所取得的成就。本书既可用于中国学生"读懂中国"的通识教育,也可作为来华留学生了解"中国文化"的绝佳素材。

感谢本书主编王革教授和其他编者,让我从书中聆听了一些新故事,也让我进一步思考该如何讲故事,认识到讲故事不仅"利于己",更是"利于人"。

李宇明

2021年4月

序于北京惧闲聊斋

Preface 前言

　　培养新时代的中国外语人才，首先要解决的就是"主流意识"和"价值观"的问题。要落实"立德树人"的教育理念，首先就需要厘清"为谁培养""为何培养""怎样培养"的根本性问题。因此，培养能讲好"中国故事"的外语人才不仅是外语学科建设的需要，也是"外语思政"背景下课程改革和教学研究的需要。

　　从课程建设的角度来看，目前国内外对"讲好中国故事"的研究多局限于传播学、叙事学和翻译学几个领域，研究方法多以内容分析和话语分析为主，缺乏对高校外语思政课程体系建设的深入研究，也缺乏"讲好中国故事"对英语学科建设内涵意义的讨论。全国高校正在贯彻落实习近平总书记关于教育的重要论述和全国教育大会的精神，贯彻落实教育部刚刚颁布实施的《高等学校课程思政建设指导纲要》。本教材的开发和建设正是基于这样的背景，帮助学生塑造正确的世界观、人生观和价值观。

编写宗旨

1. 将语言能力的拓展与"讲好中国故事"相结合，提升高校学生的外语应用能力、跨文化交际能力和国际文化传播能力；

2. 搭建课程思政建设的理想平台，贯彻"立德树人"的高校建设指导思想；

3. 助力实现高校"价值塑造、知识传授和能力培养"的人才培养目标。

教材特色

1. 充分反映了《大学英语教学指南》和《外国语言文学类教学质量国家标准》对新时代大学生人文素养培养的要求；

2. 囊括教育全球化、跨文化交流、中国生态、中国美食、中国教育、中国家庭、中国电影、中国网红等主题，兼具时代性、趣味性与实用性；

3. 以单元主题为主线，让学生通过阅读思辨、书面表达和项目实施等多样化练习，培养其中国题材英语材料的翻译能力和中国元素的英语表达能力；

4. 各单元 Text A 和 Text B 均配有短语表达和文化注释，有助于学生了解相关文化背景、掌握中英双语表达。

本教材得到了中南财经政法大学教务部的大力支持，是2019年中南财经政法大学"读懂中国"系列通识课及教材建设的成果之一。编写过程中，也得到了中南财经政法大学外国语学院广大同仁的支持和鼓励。北京语言大学李宇明教授欣然为之作序，体现了国内语言学界对"讲好中国故事"的关注和希望。在此，我代表本教材的编写团队，向北京语言大学李宇明教授、清华大学出版社外语分社郝建华分社长和责任编辑倪雅莉女士致以诚挚的谢意。

王 革

2021 年 4 月

于中南财经政法大学晓南湖

Contents / 目录

Unit 1 The Internationalization of China's Higher Education 1

Text A Shoulder Your Important Missions and
Contribute Your Youth and Talent 2
Text B China Surpasses Western Government African University
Scholarships 8
Text C American Professor Tells Wonderful Stories of China to the World 13

Unit 2 Cross-cultural Ambassadors 15

Text A Barrow Boy 16
Text B Robin (Fei Fei)—The Best Student I Never Had 22
Text C Ask an Expat: Living in Shanghai, China
A Thriving Metropolis Where East Meets West 27

Unit 3 Chinese Ecosystem 31

Text A 9 Stranded Whales Saved in East China in Dramatic Rescue by
Officers and Fishermen, Broadcast Live Online 32
Text B Elephants' 500 km-trek Across China Baffles Scientists 37
Text C Biodiversity Conservation in China Has Improved but More Efforts
Are Needed 43

Unit 4 Chinese Food 47

Text A *A Bite of China*: The Finest Food TV Ever? 48
Text B To the People, Food Is Heaven 53
Text C The Chinese Tea Ceremony: A Fascinating Ritual 59

Unit 5 Education in China 63

Text A Getting to Know Your Teacher 64
Text B Should All Countries Use the Shanghai Maths Method? 68
Text C China's English Language Ranking Improves 74

Unit 6 Chinese Families 77

Text A Conflicted Confucians 78
Text B One Child or Two? That Is the Question 82
Text C Chinese Parents Are Always Watching 87

Unit 7 Chinese Movies and Domestic Movie Market 89

Text A Weak Tea Doesn't Sell 90
Text B Why *Star Wars* Keeps Bombing in China 95
Text C China Challenges Hollywood with Own Sci-fi Blockbuster 100

Unit 8 Chinese Online Celebrities 103

Text A China's Viral Idol: A Girl Next Door with Fast-Talking Attitude 104
Text B The Reclusive Food Celebrity Li Ziqi Is My Quarantine Queen 110
Text C Brands Turn to China's Digital Influencers to Fuel Sales 115

References 119
Appendix 1 Keys to Exercises 121
Appendix 2 Suggested Translation 137

Unit 1

The Internationalization of China's Higher Education

导读

  对中国而言，高等教育国际化包括两层含义：一是中国学生走向世界，学习发达国家和地区的先进的科学文化知识、管理和社会服务经验，成为国家建设和发展的储备人才；二是吸引海外留学生到中国高校进行学习和交流。无论是哪种形式的国际化，都体现了中国在文明互鉴、文化融通、友谊建构方面的良好意愿。在本单元的几篇文章中，大家可以体会到高等教育国际化为中国和世界勾勒的美好图景。

Text A

Shoulder Your Important Missions and Contribute Your Youth and Talent

Speech by H.E. Ambassador Liu Xiaoming at the Award Ceremony of 2019 Chinese Government Award for Outstanding Self-financed Students

Chinese Embassy in the UK, 10 June, 2020

Dear teachers and students,

Good morning!

It is a real delight to join you at the Award Ceremony of 2019 Chinese Government Award for Outstanding Self-financed Students Abroad. On behalf of the Chinese Embassy in the UK and the Consulates-General in Manchester, Edinburgh and Belfast, let me begin by extending my warmest congratulations to this year's 47 outstanding awardees! I would also like to express my heartfelt thanks to all the teachers for the excellent guidance you have given to the awardees!

I have never missed this annual event since I became Chinese Ambassador to the UK. This is the 11th time in a special year. Due to COVID-19, this is the first time we confer the OSSA Award online.

The outbreak of COVID-19 has not just changed our way of communication. It has also posed severe challenges to human society, made a huge impact on the world economy and exerted a profound influence on the international landscape. It reminds us that all mankind share weal and woe in this global crisis. We all belong to a community with a shared future. It is fair to say that now, more than ever before, we need capable young people with a responsible spirit to advance the progress of mankind, to realize the rejuvenation of the Chinese nation, and to promote the steady and sustained development of China-UK relations. Against this background, today's award ceremony bears special significance. I think it reminds our young students of the three missions you have on your shoulders.

First, you shoulder the mission of promoting the progress of mankind. Replying to a letter from representatives of science workers last month President Xi Jinping said, "Innovation is the primary driving force for development, and science and technology are powerful weapons against difficulties."

Addressing global challenges and promoting the constant progress of mankind have always been an important mission for science and technology, and its success lies in scientific and technological innovation. Right now, scientists from all over the world are working day and night on medicines, vaccine, preventive technologies and testing methods that will help mankind beat COVID-19. The hope of an early breakthrough lies in scientific and technological innovation. The hope of mankind for win-win cooperation and sustainable development also lies in scientific and technological innovation. I would expect our young students to keep in mind this mission and seize the opportunities to take part in scientific and technological innovation, enhance exchanges and share outcomes, so that science and technology could provide new impetus for the prosperity in the world and play a bigger role in the progress of mankind.

Second, you shoulder the mission of realizing national rejuvenation. The Chinese nation values patriotism. Serving the motherland is regarded as the foundation of all endeavor and highest ambition in life. In the past 70 plus years since the founding of the People's Republic of China, our nation has achieved independence, grown prosperous and become strong. We are now embarking on a new journey of building a great modern socialist country in all aspects. This year, we will achieve the first centenary goal, namely, to complete the building of a moderately prosperous society in all aspects and eliminate absolute poverty. This will be a major landmark in China's history. Where the young people are ambitious, capable and responsible, the country will have a future and the nation will have hope. To realize the Chinese Dream of national rejuvenation, we need successive generations of young people to make persistent and tireless efforts. I hope you will carry on the glorious tradition of patriotism. I hope you will always live your personal dreams in the greater cause of striving for the Chinese Dream of national rejuvenation. I hope with what you have learnt here and now, you could serve your motherland and people in the future. And I hope your youthful vigour will drive you on as you work harder to realize your dream.

Third, you shoulder the mission of deepening China-UK relationship. Since it was launched by the China Scholarship Council, OSSA Award has been conferred on 509 students from about 70 British universities. You are outstanding representatives of the 220,000 Chinese students in the UK. Wherever your future takes you, whether it is academia, education, science and technology or business, I look forward to your contribution to China-UK exchanges and cooperation. In 2017, under the support of the Chinese Embassy in the UK, OSSA awardees in the UK took the initiative to set up the world's first association of their own, ASOSA-UK. Early this year when COVID-19 broke out, the association acted quickly to raise funds to purchase medical supplies for Hubei. When the epidemic broke out here in the UK, ASOSA-UK actively supported the work of the Embassy in inviting medical experts to online lectures on epidemic prevention and medical consultation. These events have been a great comfort and encouragement to students and scholars here in the UK and boosted their morale in carrying on their study and work. With love and kindness, you have built a bridge of mutual assistance between China and the UK.

China and the UK differ in social system, history, culture and development stage. But our two countries are both great civilisations with numerous talents and profound culture. Having lived and worked in this country for more than 10 years, I could feel the enormous enthusiasm of the British people to learn more about China. However, I also have to deal with frequently the bias and distortion of some politicians and media with regard to China. Telling China's stories well and making sure our message is heard remains a daunting task. You have the advantage of having studied in both China and the West. I hope you will leverage your strength to bridge the cultural gap, to tear down ideological fences, and to help extend the reach of China's stories and the stories of China-UK cooperation.

President Xi Jinping said, "Great deeds emerge from great courage and profound sense of responsibility." I hope you will keep your motherland in mind while embracing the world. I urge you to aim high, keep seeking truth and shoulder your important missions. I am sure you will contribute your youthful vigour and talent to promoting the friendly cooperation between China and other countries, and to the building of a community with a shared future for mankind!

Thank you!

 Words and Expressions

1. Self-financed Students Abroad 自费留学生
2. confer: to give sth. to sb. 授予，给予
3. weal and woe 福祸、休戚、甘苦
4. a community with a shared future 命运共同体
5. realize the rejuvenation of the Chinese nation 实现中华民族的伟大复兴
6. impetus: an influence that makes something happen or makes it happen more quickly 推动力
7. endeavor: effort 努力
8. embark on a new journey 开启新征程
9. complete the building of a moderately prosperous society in all aspects 全面建成小康社会
10. boost morale 鼓舞士气
11. daunting task 艰巨的任务
12. leverage: influence that you can use to make people do what you want 优势、影响力
13. tear down ideological fences 拆除意识形态的樊篱

Unit 1 The Internationalization of China's Higher Education

 Cultural Notes

1. **Liu Xiaoming:** China's current ambassador to the United Kingdom 刘晓明（中国现任驻英国大使）

2. **Chinese Government Award for Outstanding Self-financed Students Abroad:** With the approval of the Ministry of Education, China Scholarship Council established this award in 2003 to reward outstanding self-funded students for their outstanding academic achievements and encourage them to return to serve the country in various forms. 国家优秀自费留学生奖学金

3. **COVID-19:** a severe respiratory disease caused by a novel coronavirus that first appeared in late 2019 and became a global pandemic. 新型冠状病毒肺炎

4. **Chinese Dream:** put forth by Chinese President Xi Jinping, it aims to build a moderately prosperous society and realize national rejuvenation. 中国梦

5. **China Scholarship Council:** the Chinese Ministry of Education's non-profit organization that provides support for international academic exchange with China and is the primary vehicle through which the Chinese government awards scholarships. CSC provides both funding for Chinese citizens and residents to study abroad, and for foreign students and scholars to study in China. 中国国家留学基金委员会

Exercises

I True or False

Read the text and make a judgment of the following statements.

1. The 2020 OSSA Award was conferred online due to COVID-19 pandemic.
2. The outbreak of COVID-19 has changed our way of communication, posed severe challenges to human society, made a huge impact on the world economy and exerted a profound influence on the international landscape.
3. The Chinese youth bear multiple missions and commitments to their home country and the world.
4. The hope of an early breakthrough of vaccine against COVID-19 pandemic lies in scientific and technological innovation.
5. Patriotism is the glorious tradition of Chinese nation in history.

II Reading Comprehension

Read the text and then answer the following questions.

1. According to Ambassador Liu's speech, what are the global challenges brought about by COVID-19?

2. From Liu's perspective, what are the three missions the self-financed students should bear?
3. How do you understand President Xi's reply letter—"Innovation is the primary driving force for development, and science and technology are powerful weapons against difficulties"?
4. What are Ambassador Liu Xiaoming's expectations on Chinese overseas students?
5. Why can't the obvious differences in social system, history, culture and development stage between the UK and China stop the two countries developing mutual beneficial relationship?

III Discussion

Discuss the following questions based on the text.

1. Why did President Xi argue that innovation is the primary driving force for development, and science and technology are powerful weapons against difficulties?
2. As two great old civilizations with numerous talents and profound culture, what can be done to deepen China-UK relationship?

IV Writing

Write an essay according to the following directions.

Currently, more and more Chinese youth choose to study abroad and some choose to receive higher education in China. *haigui* (海归) refers to a returnee experiencing career success, and *haidai* (海待) relates to returnees who cannot find a secure job upon return. What do you think about the value of studying abroad or in your home country? Write an essay in no less than 250 words.

V Translation

Translate the following passage from English to Chinese.

The President said CGTN should be culturally confident, news-focused, audience-aware, and to use integrated media. CGTN should tell true stories about China and spread China's voice well, enable the world to see a multidimensional and colorful China, present China as a builder of world peace, a contributor to global development, and an upholder of international order; it should make efforts to build a community of common destiny, as Xi said. Liu Yunshan (刘云山), a member of the Standing Committee of the Political Bureau of the Communist Party of China (CPC) Central Committee, said CGTN should take responsibility for bridging China with the world. He also suggested that CGTN should put news content first, highlight new ideas and strategies of state governance with Xi as the core, tell stories about China's development, explain

China's path, theory and contribution, and have a voice in major global affairs and international issues.

Project

Work in groups and trace the life histories of winners of the State Preeminent Science and Technology Award (国家科学技术奖) and report their stories of overseas study or research. Then tell the stories you have collected in class.

Text B

China Surpasses Western Government African University Scholarships

By Andrew Jack

China's government is offering more university scholarships to African students than the leading Western governments combined, which is a sign of Beijing's use of "soft power" alongside economic investment.

The annual Global Education Monitoring Report produced by UNESCO showed China was set to offer 12,000 scholarships to African students in the coming academic year, largely to support study at Chinese universities. South Africa and Russia are also providing thousands of scholarships to African students, according to data collected before the coronavirus pandemic struck, while India and Turkey are offering growing numbers.

The UK government offers about 1,100 annual scholarships for African students, mainly through the Chevening Scholarship, while the German and French governments offer about 600 each and EU programmes over 300 more. Other European and Western governments provide smaller support.

Simon Marginson, professor of higher education at Oxford university, said the trend reflected China's efforts at soft diplomacy linked to its Belt and Road Initiative that has led it to pump billions of dollars into infrastructure projects around the world, including in Africa. "China's aid is regionally specific and tends to be defined by the Belt and Road," he said. "One feature of Chinese policy, compared with the UK, is long-term continuity." In the UK, he said there was a tendency to "shift policy from budget to budget and more so if there is a change of government. But China can be expected to keep increasing scholarships for African students for many years to come".

The UK, France and Germany and other Western donors tend to focus the bulk of their educational aid budget on supporting projects for school-age children. The UNESCO data cover official government-backed programmes and not support from individual universities. Two corporate-backed providers also have a strong presence in supporting African students. ABSA, the bank, and the MasterCard Foundation, the charitable arm of the payments group, are among the leading providers of university-level scholarships.

The UNESCO analysis highlights that most scholarships go to support university places in the funding countries rather than providing students with places in African universities, which would help strengthen the institutions. It also highlights that while scholarship providers typically track whether beneficiaries complete their courses, most share little information on criteria and frequently do not include verifiable metrics or have objectives to recruit those from disadvantaged backgrounds. To remedy this, observers have called for scholarships to be modified to enhance social mobility for talented African students and to develop the continent's own education system.

Patrick Dunne, chair of Education Sub-Saharan Africa, a charity supporting tertiary education on the continent, which helped analyze the data, said: "The game needs to change on the way people think about scholarships. We could get a lot more bangs for our buck. If there is much more focus on the impact, there will be more money flowing into scholarships and we will be able to see the return." He called for a more systematic system to connect eligible school students in most need with scholarships to give them access to better educational opportunities.

Kenneth King, professor emeritus at Edinburgh University, stressed that while China's policy was to use soft power to build long-term influence, its universities "don't spend a lot of time keeping in touch with people who've been there". He contrasted this approach with the significant fundraising-linked efforts in Western universities to cultivate alumni networks.

Words and Expressions

1. **pandemic:** a disease that spreads over a country or the whole world 全国或全球大流行病
2. **beneficiary:** a person who gains as a result of sth. 受益者
3. **verifiable:** can be proved to be true or genuine 可证实的
4. **metric:** a standard of measurement 尺度、标准
5. **remedy:** successful way of dealing with a problem, treatment 补救办法
6. **enhance:** to improve quality, value or attractiveness 增进

Cultural Notes

1. **soft diplomacy:** Typically, it's a term that refers to attempts to engage directly with the public in round-about ways; it's diplomacy's soft power equivalent in that the goal isn't really about accomplishing a particular substantive task as much as it is to try and alter the fundamental basis under which a diplomatic relationship exists between countries. 软外交
2. **soft power:** the ability to attract and co-opt, rather than coerce. In other words, soft power involves shaping the preferences of others through appeal and attraction. A defining

feature of soft power is that it is non-coercive; the currency of soft power includes culture, political values, and foreign policies. 软实力

3. **UNESCO:** the United Nations Educational, Scientific and Cultural Organization. It seeks to build peace through international cooperation in education, the sciences and culture. UNESCO's programmes contribute to the achievement of the Sustainable Development Goals defined in Agenda 2030, adopted by the UN General Assembly in 2015. 联合国教科文组织

4. **Chevening Scholarship:** It enables outstanding emerging leaders from all over the world to pursue one-year master's degrees in the UK. 志奋领奖学金

5. **Simon Marginson:** Professor of Higher Education at the University of Oxford, Director of the ESRC/OFSRE Centre for Global Higher Education (CGHE), and Editor-in-Chief of the journal *Higher Education*. 西蒙·马金森

6. **The Belt and Road Initiative:** It refers to the Initiative, proposed by Chinese President Xi Jinping, consisting of the Silk Road Economic Belt and the 21st-Century Maritime Silk Road, and aiming to boost connectivity along and beyond the routes of the ancient Silk Road. With a view to enhancing both China's development and its cooperation with global partners, it focuses on cementing links in five key areas: policies, infrastructure, trade, finance and people-to-people bonds. "一带一路"倡议

7. **ABSA:** Amalgamated Banks of South Africa, a consolidated merger of numerous financial institutions established in 1991 南部非洲联合银行

8. **The MasterCard Foundation:** an international non-governmental organization established by MasterCard in 2006. The foundation develops programs primarily in education, employment and agriculture fields. 万事达基金会

9. **Education Sub-Saharan Africa:** a charity supporting tertiary education on the continent 非洲撒哈拉教育

Exercises

I True or False

Read the text and make a judgment of the following statements.

1. China has surpassed many leading Western governments in offering more university scholarships to African students.
2. Compared with China, the UK government is the second largest scholarships sponsor for African students.
3. There was a tendency to "shift policy from budget to budget" due to the change of the UK government.
4. Chinese universities did not keep in frequent touch with the African students who had studied in China.

5. Patrick Dunne, chair of Education Sub-Saharan Africa, a charity supporting tertiary education on the continent, argued that the way people think about scholarships should be changed.

II Reading Comprehension

Read the text and then answer the following questions.

1. As for African university students, who are the scholarship providers for African students apart from China?
2. Compared with the UK and other Western countries, what is the advantage of Chinese funding system for African students?
3. How do you understand the phrase "long-term continuity" in Paragraph 4?
4. Why did the observers argue that scholarships should be modified to enhance social mobility for talented African students and to develop the continent's own education system?
5. What are the differences between Chinese and Western donors in supporting African students?

III Discussion

Discuss the following questions based on the text.

1. What is the significance for China to surpass Western government in offering African scholarships?
2. To facilitate the Belt and Road Initiative, what reforms shall be made in the scholarship policy towards the African students?

IV Writing

Write an essay according to the following directions.

In China, most international students come from the developing countries in Southeast Asia or Africa. Conduct a survey and write an essay about the advantages of studying in China. You are expected to write an essay in no less than 250 words with a clear structure and strong supporting evidence.

V Translation

Translate the following passage from English to Chinese.

Decades of economic development have enabled China's leaders to modernize the country's education and transformed China into a hub for international students. Whereas foreign students

historically only traveled to China for language courses, students from around the world are increasingly drawn to China to enroll in technical courses and attain professional degrees. China's economic boom has also created new opportunities for middle-class families to send their children to study abroad. Cultivating talent both at home and abroad will be critical for Chinese leaders as they push for an innovation-based economy driven by a well-educated workforce.

VI Project

Work in groups and track the African leaders or celebrities who once studied in China and have made contribution to their own countries. Report your findings in your class.

Text C

American Professor Tells Wonderful Stories of China to the World

By Hong Yu

William Brown, a business professor from Xiamen University is an American, but has been engaged in telling wonderful stories about China to the world. For him, the progress made by China can be called a miracle.

Brown came to China in the 1970s to learn Chinese out of curiosity. In 1988, he became a foreign teacher in Xiamen University, and in 1993 he received a Friendship Award from the Chinese government.

During his time at Xiamen University, Brown established a close relationship with the students and made many contributions to the business administration project of Xiamen University. Brown bought a tricycle and, in his spare time, took his whole family around Xiamen. He often communicated with locals to learn about the city's culture and stories. He noticed that in the late 1980s, Xiamen's economy and urban construction began to develop rapidly, while paying attention to the protection of natural ecology.

In 1994, he went on a 40,000-kilometer journey covering more than half of China with his wife and children, which lasted for three months. In 2019, he set out again, traveling tens of thousands of kilometers for 31 days to explore the great developments and changes that had taken place in various parts of China.

These two trips left him amazed about China's achievements in the past 70 years since the founding of the People's Republic of China, and how these magical changes have benefited every Chinese. For Brown, Chinese people's living standards have improved significantly, and their happiness is increasing with each passing day. He believes that there are many successful experiences that can be used as reference by other countries. The progress made by China can be called a miracle, especially in the more than 40 years of reform and opening up.

A number of projects carried out by China in various fields have attracted worldwide attention, such as the Three Gorges Project and the South-North Water Transfer Project. Brown is increasingly impressed by China's determination and efforts to get rid of poverty. Today, infrastructure such as electricity and transportation in remote areas and rural areas of China has been greatly improved.

Xiamen obtained the title of International Garden City in 2002. At that time, as a

representative, he told the story of the harmonious cohabitation between Xiamen people and nature. Brown believed that China attaches great importance to green development and has strong executive power.

During his more than 30 years of living in China, Brown has persisted in studying Chinese history, listening to Chinese stories, and spreading them to the world. Since 2000, he has been writing books to introduce China overseas in order to help more Chinese and foreign readers understand Xiamen and Fujian.

In December 2018, *Off the Wall—How We Fell for China*, written by Brown, was published. The book is a collection of 47 letters he had written to his family since 1988. In the book, he used interesting stories and humorous expressions to show the pleasing changes that have taken place in China's economic and social landscape.

"I am full of love for Xiamen and China. China has already become my second home. I will always be a storyteller of China and continue to share more wonderful Chinese stories with the world," said Brown.

Unit 2

Cross-cultural Ambassadors

导读

　　改革开放四十多年以来，中国经历了怎样深刻的政治和社会经济的变革？社会生活又发生了怎样天翻地覆的变化？通过"街头小贩"的英语学习史、美国外教的"家书"，以及定居上海的澳大利亚旅居者的描述，相信大家都可以从本单元的几篇文章中找到答案。

Text A

Barrow Boy

By Duncan Clark

Jack Ma was born on September 10, 1964, the Year of the Dragon, in Hangzhou, a city one hundred miles to the southwest of Shanghai. His parents named him "Yun", meaning "cloud". His surname, "Ma", is the same as the Chinese word for "horse".

As a boy, Jack fell in love with the English language and literature, particularly readings of Mark Twain's *The Adventures of Tom Sawyer* which he listened to on a shortwave radio. Later it was the arrival of foreign tourists in China that provided Jack with his opening to the outside world. In late 1978, when Jack was fourteen, China launched the reform and opening up policy, in pursuit of foreign trade and investment. After a decade of turmoil the country was on the verge of bankruptcy, and desperately needed hard currency.

In 1978, only 728 foreign tourists visited Hangzhou. But the following year more than forty thousand came to the city. Jack relished any opportunity to practice his English. He started waking up before dawn and riding his bicycle for forty minutes to the Hangzhou Hotel to greet foreign tourists.

As he recalled, "Every morning from five o'clock I would read English in front of the hotel. A lot of foreign visitors came from the USA, from Europe. I'd give them a free tour of West Lake, and they taught me English. For nine years! And I practiced my English every morning, no matter if it snowed or rained."

An American tourist whose father and husband were named Jack suggested the name and Ma Yun became known in English henceforth as Jack. He is dismissive of the quality of his English: "I just make myself understood. The grammar is terrible." But Jack never dismisses how much learning the language has helped him in life: "English helps me a lot. It makes me understand the world better, helps me to meet the best CEOs and leaders in the world, and makes me understand the distance between China and the world."

Among the many tourists who came to Hangzhou in 1980 was an Australian family, the Morleys. Ken Morley, a recently retired electrical engineer, had signed up for a tour of China offered by the local branch of the Australia China Friendship Society. He took along his wife, Judy, and their three children, David, Stephen, and Susan, for whom it would be their first overseas trip. For Jack, their visit would change his life.

Today, David runs a yoga studio in Australia, where I managed to track him down. He kindly shared his memories and the photos of his family's visit to China and their enduring friendship with Jack.

On July 1, 1980, the Morleys' Australian tour group arrived by plane in Hangzhou from Beijing and was transferred by bus to the Shangri-La Hotel on West Lake, the same hotel (then the Hangzhou Hotel) where President Nixon and his entourage had stayed eight years earlier. David recalls being shown the suite where the First Couple had stayed, allocated to their tour leader, complete with "plush, red velvet toilet seats, which we three children were fascinated by".

The next day the Australian group's itinerary included a boat trip on West Lake, followed by a visit to the nearby tea plantations and on to the Liuhe (Six Harmonies) Pagoda before returning to the hotel for dinner at 6:30 p.m. Taking advantage of the "free evening", David and a young woman called Keva whom he had befriended on the trip snuck across the road from the hotel to the park opposite, overlooking West Lake. There they proceeded to play with matches, practicing the art of "match flicking" that she had taught him. This involved standing a match upside-down with its head on the striking surface and flicking it with your fingers and watching it spiral off to, David recalls, "hopefully an uneventful extinguishment." Fortunately that day, the park didn't catch fire. But David and Keva's antics did catch the attention of a fifteen-year-old boy—Jack Ma. David recalls, "It was on that free evening, flicking matches in the park, that I was approached by a young man wanting to try his newly acquired English skills on me. He introduced himself; we swapped pleasantries and agreed to meet in the park again."

On July 4, their last day in Hangzhou, David introduced Jack to his sister, Susan, and invited him and some other local children to play Frisbee with them in the park. David described the scene to me:

Marking out a playing area with shoes and other items, "we were soon surrounded by hundreds of Chinese spectators." Jack's father, Ma Laifa, took photos of the game.

David's father, Ken Morley, once described his first impressions of Jack as a "barrow boy", or a street hawker. "He really wanted to practice his English, and he was very friendly. Our kids were very impressed."

David described how the family stayed in touch: "What followed that meeting was a pen pal relationship that I kept up for a few years until my father started to take an interest in helping this young man." Jack would correspond regularly with Ken, referring to him as "Dad", who asked him to "double space his letters so that any corrections could be sent back in the spaces". David explained, "The original with corrections was returned for learning purposes with the reply letter. I believe this greatly helped and encouraged Jack to continue with his English studies."

Armed with his improving English, rich knowledge of the history of the area, and a knack for storytelling, Jack embraced the opportunity to show more foreign tourists around the sights of West Lake. He relished visiting Hangzhou's teahouses, where locals would play Chinese chess and cards and recount "tall tales".

Jack would often accompany his grandmother to Buddhist temples to burn incense and worship the gods. He developed a passion for *tai chi* and reading *The Water Margin,* a classic Chinese tale that features 108 heroes—the number of employees he later would set as an early head count target for Alibaba.

Words and Expressions

1. **barrow:** a small open vehicle with two wheels from which fruit, vegetables, etc. are sold in the street 两轮流动售货车（售卖水果蔬菜等常用）
2. **turmoil:** a state of great anxiety and confusion, disorder, uncertainty 混乱，动荡，恐慌
3. **dismissive:** showing that you do not believe a person or thing to be important or worth considering 轻蔑的，鄙视的
4. **relish:** to get great pleasure from sth., to want very much to do sth. 享受，获得乐趣
5. **dismissive:** if you are dismissive of sb. or sth., you say or show that you think they are not important or have no value. 拒绝考虑，对……轻视的，鄙视的
6. **sign up:** if you sign up for an organization, you sign a contract officially agreeing to do a job or course of study 签约，雇佣，报名
7. **track down:** to pursue for food or sport (as of wild animals) 追捕，查出，找到
8. **entourage:** a group of people who travel with an important person （统称）随行人员，随从
9. **fascinate:** to attract sb.'s interest very much 深深吸引，迷住
10. **itinerary:** a plan of a journey, including the route and the places that you visit 行程，旅行日程
11. **spiral off:** to decrease rapidly 急剧减少
12. **antics:** behavior which is silly and funny in a way that people usually like 滑稽可笑的举止
13. **flick:** to hit sth. with a sudden quick movement, especially using your finger and thumb together, or your hand 轻击，轻拍，轻拂，轻弹
14. **swap:** to give sth. to sb. and receive sth. in exchange 交换（东西）
15. **pleasantry:** a friendly remark made in order to be polite 客气话，客套
16. **Frisbee:** a light plastic object, shaped like a plate, that is thrown from one player to another in a game 弗里斯比飞盘（投掷游戏用的飞碟）

17. recount: to tell sb. about sth., especially sth. that you have experienced 讲述

18. tall tale: an improbable (unusual or incredible of fanciful) story 荒诞不经的故事

Cultural Notes

1. **The Year of the Dragon:** The Dragon (simplified Chinese: 龙; traditional Chinese: 龍) is the fifth of the 12-year cycle of animals which appear in the Chinese zodiac related to the Chinese calendar. 龙年

2. **Mark Twain:** pseudonym of Samuel Langhorne Clemens, (born on November 30, 1835, Florida, Missouri, U.S.–died on April 21, 1910, Redding, Connecticut), American humorist, journalist, lecturer, and novelist who acquired international fame for his travel narratives. A gifted raconteur, distinctive humorist, and irascible moralist, he transcended the apparent limitations of his origins to become a popular public figure and one of America's best and most beloved writers. 马克·吐温

3. *The Adventures of Tom Sawyer:* Tom Sawyer, fictional character, the young protagonist of *The Adventures of Tom Sawyer* (1876) by Mark Twain. Considered the epitome of the all-American boy, Tom Sawyer is full of mischief but basically pure-hearted. He is probably best remembered for the incident in which he gets a number of other boys to whitewash his Aunt Polly's fence—an unpleasant task in his eyes—by making the work seem to be extremely absorbing.《汤姆·索亚历险记》

4. **West Lake:** It is a freshwater lake in Hangzhou, China. It is divided into five sections by three causeways. West Lake has influenced poets and painters throughout Chinese history for its natural beauty and historic relics, and it has also been among the most important sources of inspiration for Chinese garden designers. It was made a UNESCO World Heritage Site in 2011, described as having "influenced garden design in the rest of China as well as Japan and Korea over the centuries" and reflecting "an idealized fusion between humans and nature". 西湖

5. **President Nixson:** Richard Nixon, in full Richard Milhous Nixon, (born on January 9, 1913, Yorba Linda, California, U.S.–died on April 22, 1994, New York, New York), 37th president of the United States (1969–1974), who, faced with almost certain impeachment for his role in the Watergate scandal, became the first American president to resign from office. He was also vice president (1953–1961) under Pres. Dwight D. Eisenhower. 尼克松总统

6. **Liuhe Pagoda:** Literally Six Harmonies Pagoda, it is a multi-story Chinese pagoda in southern Hangzhou, Zhejiang Province, China. It is located at the foot of Yuelun Hill, facing the Qiantang River. It was originally constructed in 970 by the Wuyue Kingdom, destroyed in 1121, and reconstructed fully by 1165, during the Southern Song Dynasty (1127–1279). 六和塔

7. *tai chi:* also *taiji*, Chinese boxing, ancient and distinctive Chinese form of exercise or attack and defense that is popular throughout the world. As exercise, *tai chi* is designed to provide

relaxation in the process of body-conditioning exercise and is drawn from the principles of *taiji*, notably including the harmonizing of the *yin* and *yang*, the passive and active principles respectively. 太极

8. ***The Water Margin*:** Also translated as *All Men Are Brothers*, *Outlaws of the Marsh*, the ancient Chinese vernacular novel is known from several widely varying manuscripts under the name *Shuihuzhuan*. Its variations are so extreme as to make the work the most textually complex in Chinese literature; the text cannot be dated with accuracy, and its authors cannot be identified. Based in part on ancient legends and oral tradition, *The Water Margin* is generally divided into simplified and fuller text versions, the earliest of which date from the early 16th century. Each manuscript within these series contains some combination of six episodic adventure tales about 108 bandit-heroes and their various campaigns. An English translation of the first 70 chapters with an abridgment of the last 30 was published as *Outlaws of the Marsh* (1981).《水浒传》

Exercises

❶ True or False

Read the text and make a judgment of the following statements.

1. It was the reform and opening-up policy that provided Ma with his opening to the outside world.
2. After a decade of turmoil China was on the verge of bankruptcy, and desperately needed hard currency.
3. Over four thousand foreign tourists visited Hangzhou in 1979.
4. English learning helped Jack Ma understand the world, meet world CEOs and leaders and above all, find the distance between China and the world.
5. Jack Ma is a business leader with the international vision and Chinese heritage.

❷ Reading Comprehension

Read the text and then answer the following questions.

1. How did Ma take any opportunity to practice his English as a teenager?
2. How did the Morleys from Australia help Ma to improve his English?
3. Why was Ma called a "barrow boy" by Ken Morley?
4. How did the experience of English learning help Ma?
5. Why was Ma so popular as an amateur free tour guide?

Ⅲ Discussion

Discuss the following questions based on the text.

1. Do you think the meeting of the Morleys changed the life of Jack Ma? If so, justify your reasons.
2. What can you learn from the story of "Barrow Boy"?

Ⅳ Writing

Write an essay according to the following directions.

In the post pandemic era, there are increasing debates on the survival of globalization. Some argue that the post COVID-19 era will decelerate even terminate globalization. What is your opinion on the future of globalization? You are required to write an essay in no less than 250 words with 3 paragraphs.

Ⅴ Translation

Translate the following passage from English to Chinese.

Jack Ma was born on September 10, 1964, into a family that lived on the shores of West Lake in Hangzhou. Ma legend has it that his family was common and ordinary, but ordinary families do not live on the shores of West Lake. Ma's mother and father spent their lives as professional performers of *pingtan*, a traditional style of storytelling and ballad singing performed in Suzhou, in southern China.

As a result of this background, Ma grew up speaking the Suzhou dialect with his parents, and he has strong attachment to the city and the traditions of that historic place. Suzhou has two kinds of people, as the saying goes: one kind loves to talk, and the other loves to listen. One does not have to look far into Ma's background to find the roots of his astonishing ability to extemporize onstage and his ability to inspire high performance through his speeches. From childhood, Ma watched and absorbed the training of professional performers, especially his parents. His own performance style may be attributed to that early exposure: Ma uses simple and direct language to explain precisely what he means. He wastes no words—and he gets to the point.

Ⅵ Project

Work in groups and find out another business leader who has changed Chinese technology or industry. Introduce this leader to your classmates in a 10-minute presentation.

Text B

Robin (Fei Fei)—The Best Student I Never Had

By William Brown

July 19th, 2007

Dear Uncle Mitch and Janet,

Ahoy from Amoy! You've shared a few times about the talented Mainland Chinese students you've had there in L.A., but I doubt you've ever taught a student like Robin (Fei Fei). Actually, she was never my student either, and never will be, now that she's headed off for a master's degree at Harvard. But I did get to co-author a book with her, which was quite an experience.

For Xiamen University's 85th anniversary, I had only two months to write the 363-page bilingual, *Xiamen University—Strength of the Nation*. A few professors offered to help but I had heard of Robin, a junior in International Business and Economics who seemed to know everyone and be involved in everything, and had won numerous scholarships and awards. I suspected if anyone on campus had the ability and stamina to help me beat the deadline, it was Robbin. And once you've read her story, you'll see why she was the best student that I never had.

I first met Robin in 2005 at a large celebration she'd helped arrange on Zhangzhou campus. Virtually every foreigner on campus had told me about her. In spite of her activities, she was first in her department every year. "Study is always my first priority," she said, "no matter how many activities I'm involved in." But given Robin's childhood experiences, I can see why she takes study so seriously.

On a sweltering summer's day, Robin's mother was in the middle of household chores when her water broke. Her husband bicycled 15 miles to the hospital with his groaning pregnant wife on back. When they arrived hours later, she was in such agony that the doctor recommended a C-section. Caesarians were so risky at that time that Robin's father had to sign many forms and waivers in case he lost mother, baby or both. Fortunately, both mother and child survived, and he named his daughter "Fei Fei", meaning "to fly" (though with the homophones/different characters).

Robin's dad was a worker in one of China's largest iron and steel factories and her mother worked in a textile factory, but seeing her humble family's background, young Robin determined to find a way to ease the financial burden on her family. Her grandfather had taught her, "Learn more and do more as long as you live," so she chose education as the path to success.

School was, at first, a lonely experience for Robin. She was too shy to make friends, and was embarrassed by her poor clothes and simple lunches. But she quickly gained attention and respect from teachers and students alike as she became top in her class—even becoming a tutor for older children.

Today, Robin excels at Xiamen University just as she did throughout her first 12 years of school. She not only speaks English like a foreigner but astounds Chinese with her flawless Mandarin and has won many competitions in both languages. She was president of XMU's Putonghua (Mandarin) Association, and producer and broadcaster for XMU's "English Café" program for two years, as well as anchorperson for XMU TV news center. Robin has written articles for *Xiamen Daily,* represented XMU in the "Model United Nations" in Beijing, and she appeared on CCTV10's "Outlook". She's hosted conferences, banquets and competitions and worked with various foreign governments, receiving a letter of commendation from the Philippine government and heartfelt appreciation from the Australians!

Yet in spite of Robin's killer schedule, she also took time to help me write a bilingual 363-page book in only 2 months. She did research, conducted interviews, wrote articles and chapters, translated from English to Chinese and back again.

What most moved me about Robin was not her work ethic but her integrity. As No.1 in her class, Robin was entitled to choose any university in China but she gave that privilege to the No. 2 student when she applied for a master's degree at Harvard. Faculty and students alike were quick to criticize her. "What if you're not accepted?"

"But if I don't give up place," she explained, "and I'm accepted abroad, it will be too late for the No. 2 student to take my place. This is the right thing to do." Fortunately for Robin, and for Harvard, she was accepted. But when she headed to the U.S. for the first time with nothing but $100 cash and two suitcases full of books, I asked, "How can you make it on $100?"

"I don't need any money," Robin replied. "I have a full scholarship and a living stipend."

I asked Robin about her goals in life and she said that in the short term, her goal was to give her parents their first plane ride and to show them how to check in. I would not be surprised if, someday, Robin bought her parents a plane. Fly, Fei Fei, Fly!

Well, Mitch and Janet, enough for this month. Write when you can; we've got cobwebs in our mailbox.

Bill, Sue, Shan, Matt and Charlemagne the cat

Words and Expressions

1. **stamina:** the physical or mental strength that enables you to do sth. difficult for long periods of time, patience 耐力，耐性，持久力

2. **sweltering** 闷热的，酷热难耐的

3. **groan:** to make a long deep sound because you are annoyed, upset or in pain, or with pleasure 呻吟，叹息，哼哼

4. **agony:** extreme physical or mental pain（精神或肉体上的）极度痛苦

5. **C-section (=caesarean=caesarian):** a medical operation in which an opening is cut in a woman's body in order to take out a baby 剖腹产术

6. **waiver:** a situation in which sb. gives up a little right or claim; an official document stating this（对合法权利或要求的）弃权，弃权说明，免责条款

7. **astound:** to surprise or shock sb. very much 使十分吃惊，使大为吃惊，使吃惊

8. **flawless:** without flaws and therefore perfect 完美的，无瑕的

9. **commendation:** (formal) praise; approval 赞扬，称赞，赞成，嘉许

10. **heartfelt:** showing strong feelings that are sincere 衷心的，真诚的

11. **killer schedule** 十分繁忙的行程

12. **integrity:** the quality of being honest and having strong moral principles 诚实正直

13. **cobweb:** a fine net of threads made by a spider to catch insects 蜘蛛网

Cultural Notes

1. **Xiamen University:** Xiamen University (XMU), established in 1921 by renowned patriotic overseas Chinese leader Mr. Tan Kah Kee, is the first university founded by an overseas Chinese in the history of modern Chinese education. XMU has long been listed among China's leading universities on the national 211 Project, 985 Project and Double First-class initiative, which have been launched by the Chinese government to support selected universities in achieving world-class standing. Xiamen University Malaysia Campus is the first overseas branch campus established by a prestigious Chinese university. 厦门大学

2. **Model United Nations:** Also known as Model UN or MUN, it is an educational simulation and academic activity in which students can learn about diplomacy, international relations, and the United Nations. MUN involves and teaches participants speaking, debating, and writing skills, in addition to critical thinking, teamwork, and leadership abilities. Usually an extracurricular activity, it is meant to engage students and allow them to develop deeper understanding into current world issues. 模拟联合国

3. **CCTV10's "Outlook":** It was launched on June 18,1999 into the CCTV 10 Science and Education Channel. It is a leisure educational program that introduces English language and culture by the education department of CCTV Social Education Program Center. The program teaches fashionable English, survival English and the expressions of Western culture. CCTV 10 中央科教频道《希望英语》

Exercises

I True or False

Read the text and make a judgment of the following statements.

1. Robin (Fei Fei) used to be the author's student and co-author of a book.
2. The author wrote a bilingual book to celebrate XMU's 85th anniversary.
3. Robin's childhood experience made her a very serious attitude towards her study.
4. Robin seems to be an all-around student with great talents in many areas.
5. Robin gave the privilege to the No. 2 student to the access to the postgraduate study because she has got an offer of Harvard Graduate School.

II Reading Comprehension

Read the text and then answer the following questions.

1. For what reasons did the author choose Robin as the co-author of the book he was writing?
2. What happened to Robin's mom when she was doing housework?
3. Why was Robin named as Fei Fei in Chinese?
4. What changes took place to Robin as a university student?
5. What was in her mind when Fei Fei left for Harvard?

III Discussion

Discuss the following questions based on the text.

1. What are the key factors that contribute to Robin's success? Support your argument with some examples.
2. What can we learn from Robin's story?

Ⅳ Writing

Write an essay according to the following directions.

Do you know or have any friends who are good at time management and are able to complete multiple tasks at the same time? An efficient person may have more opportunities. If you agree, write an essay in no less than 250 words.

Ⅴ Translation

Translate the following passage from English to Chinese.

I would never forget how excited I was when I got the phone call from the Embassy of China in Sweden notifying me that I got this award. It is one of greatest moments in my life. Being granted this award means my scientific research development and accomplishment during my PhD study period is recognized on an outstanding level by the Chinese government from a professional point of view. Hence, I feel very proud and honoured to be able to get this award. Most importantly, I am sincerely grateful to my supervisor Professor Erik Renström and my co-supervisor associate professor Enming Zhang for their tremendous encouragement, help, support and guidance, which are endless throughout my PhD study journey. I would never get this award without their supervision. I would also like to thank Lund University to provide me a wonderful platform to develop myself.

Ⅵ Project

Work in groups and find out some contemporary Chinese who stand out from the rag to rich. Make a 10-minute presentation of his or her stories in English in class.

Text C

Ask an Expat: Living in Shanghai, China
A Thriving Metropolis Where East Meets West

By Donna Campbell

Often considered to be China's most sophisticated city, Shanghai is a modern upstart that is characterized by its fascinating mix of East and West. Often referred to as the "City on the Sea", Shanghai is exotic and commercial, modern and old-fashioned, progressive and regressive—all at the same time.

Today Shanghai attracts expats from all over the world and the total number of foreigners living in the city is forecast to be over 800,000 by the year 2020.

Expat life in Shanghai is never dull. The city offers dizzying skyscrapers, a diverse night scene, endless shopping opportunities and some of the best restaurants in the world.

Expat Interviews: Keeping Sane in Shanghai

Today we meet Donna Campbell, an Australian who is living in Shanghai, China. Donna shares her story with us, describing how she finds life in China, why you need to be careful crossing the road and how you can stop yourself from going crazy in a city that is so culturally different from your home country.

Q: Where are you currently living?

A: Shanghai, China.

Q: Where were you born?

A: Townsville, Australia.

Q: Why did you move overseas and why did you choose your host country?

A: I first visited Shanghai in the late 1990s with a group of Australian travel writers and fell in love with the city for its sheer size and buzz so I knew what to expect. My job in Australia was Regional PR and Special Events Manager for Conrad Treasury and Conrad Jupiters hotels and casinos and while it was definitely one of the best jobs in Australia, after 11 years I was looking for a new challenge. I was fortunate enough to be recommended by a friend for a role for the JW Marriott hotel in Shanghai and after 2 long distance phone interviews I was offered the job.

Hence in the matter of 3 weeks I had sold my car, rented out my apartment and packed

up all my belongings to move to China. It was quite daunting at first, as I arrived on my own (I am single) the week before Christmas not knowing one person and not being able to speak the language. Also Christmas Day is a normal work day here in China, so I came from 35 degrees Celsius, white sandy beaches and blue skies of Australia to minus 6 degrees, snow and winter.

Q: How long have you been living in your host country?

A: This is my second time in China. I was here from 2006 to 2009 the first time, then moved back to Australia briefly (1 year exactly) to take up a new role in Melbourne, Australia but I missed expat life. Hence I was offered a chance to come back to Shanghai to open up the new The Langham Xintiandi hotel, so I moved back in July 2010.

Q: Who did you relocate with?

A: I came alone.

Q: Was it hard to get a visa for your host country that was appropriate to your circumstances?

A: Since I was offered the role with Langham, they arranged everything on my behalf. Prior to moving I had to have some medical checks back in Australia, but the whole process runs very smoothly here in Shanghai. Once you get here you again have to go to a hospital and there are a series of general health tests that you have to undergo, which usually only takes around 2 hours. Also most companies use the services of a professional agency that arranges the meetings with the immigration bureau. In most cases everything runs very efficiently. Also since I am on a single package it is much easier than if you have a family as they also have to undergo all the medical tests.

Q: How do you make your living in your host country?

A: I work as Director of Communications for the Langham Xintiandi, a five-star luxury hotel located in the heart of Shanghai's Xintiandi entertainment district. My role involves media relations, public relations, marketing communications, advertising and special events.

Q: Do you speak the local language and do you think it's important to speak the local language?

A: While I am certainly not fluent I do have enough Mandarin to get by, when I was here the first time I was taking weekly language classes and my staff also teach me one new word/sentence each day. The first thing you learn is to communicate with taxi drivers as they don't speak English at all. Then so long as you have enough words to communicate with your *ayi* (housekeeper) and shop at the local market then it is pretty easy to get by. Most of the younger Chinese generation (under 40) speak English as they are taught from a very early age at school. In fact most expats are lazy and do not bother to learn even the basics, which I find is an insult to the Chinese as we are guests in their country, and if they come to our country then we expect them to learn English.

Q: Do you ever get homesick?

A: I do miss the beaches, blue sky and clean air of Australia; however, I don't miss the fact that everything shuts at 5 p.m. in Australia. I love the fact that just about everything is open/available 24/7 here in Shanghai. I was back in Australia last week for a holiday and while I did enjoy the beach, I found the pace a bit too slow and quiet compared with Shanghai. Most "comfort" Australian or Western foods are also available here in Shanghai you just pay a little extra for them. I have started writing a blog about my experiences about living in Shanghai.

Q: How long do you plan to remain in your host country?

A: I have another 18 months to go on my contract so I do plan to be here for some time yet.

Q: Have you purchased a property in your host country or do you rent?

A: My accommodation is included as part of my remuneration package, which is the case with most expats. I live very close to my work in an apartment compound that has a gym, swimming pool and supermarket all located within the compound.

Q: What is the cost of housing like in your host country?

A: It is much more difficult to purchase property here in China for expats. You have to be living here for 12 months first and then you also have to hold on to the property for 5 years before you can sell it. I have definitely seen the price of both rental accommodation and real estate increase over the past 5 years. Average rental prices for 2-bedroom apartment range from around RMB12,000 up to RMB20,000 per month and most usually come fully furnished. The first time I moved all my furniture up to Shanghai but it was not necessary; this time I have left most of my furniture in storage in Australia and just bought the necessities up with me.

Q: What is the cost of living like in your host country?

A: If you live like a local i.e. shop at the local fruit and vegetable markets it is extremely cheap with an average shop for 2 people costing around RMB50 per week; taxis are also very cheap with most journeys costing around RMB14. Most expats have an *ayi* (housekeeper) which costs around RMB30–RMB50 per hour. I also love the fact that spa treatments and beauty services are extremely cheap, I have my hair blow-dried twice a week for RMB50. On the flip side if you live like an expat i.e. eating out every night at high end international restaurants and shop at Western food supermarkets it can be quite expensive, as with every international city.

Q: What do you think about the locals?

A: The Chinese people are very accommodating if you are respectful. If you come here thinking that you know better than them or try to impose your culture/expectations on them then only you will suffer. It is very easy to make new friends here in Shanghai whether they are locals or fellow expats, people are very embracing of new people and tend to take you under their wing and keen to introduce you to the local market, "where to shop" tips, etc. Always remember there are 1.3 billion people in China and only a few thousand expats.

Q: What are the three things you like the most about your host country?

A:

1. The fact that just about everything is open 24 hours a day, 7 days a week.

2. The great selection of cuisines from regional Chinese to every international cuisine that you have come to know.

3. The variety of people that visit—whenever you go out you meet new people from all around the world.

Q: What are the three things you like the least?

A:

1. The winters in Shanghai can be depressing (coming from Australia) we have just had a very long winter (6 months) I am looking forward to spring and summer which are the ideal times to visit.

2. Sometimes the pace of the city takes its toll—you do need to get out of the city every 2 or 3 months for a break just to clear your head.

3. The pollution and smog also take their toll—I miss clear skies and especially seeing stars at night time.

Q: Do you have any tips for our readers about living in your host country?

A: Embrace the culture and don't try to change it—come with the right attitude and look at the big picture that you are in one of the oldest and richest and diverse cultural countries in the world. Get out and explore the city and get to know the locals. Don't just mingle with other expats.

Unit 3

Chinese Ecosystem

导读

2020年年初，一队野生亚洲象从云南西双版纳栖息地开始北上，2021年4月首次现身云南玉溪市，并一路向北抵近昆明。一时间，"一路象北"引起了中外专家学者和普通大众的高度关注；同年7月，12头瓜头鲸在浙江临海搁浅，其中9头在当地政府、救援人员和附近居民的共同努力之下获救，整个救援过程进行了网络直播。不论是云南野生象群不明原因的出走还是中国海域鲸鱼的频现，都与中国生态环境的变化有着千丝万缕的关系。本单元将带你领略中国新生态观之下中国社会与野生动物的和谐共存。

Text A

9 Stranded Whales Saved in East China in Dramatic Rescue by Officers and Fishermen, Broadcast Live Online

By Cui Fandi

Nine of the 12 melon-headed whales stranded on the coast in East China have been rescued through the joint efforts of local officers, rescuers and residents racing against time, as millions of netizens witnessed the process in a live video broadcast.

By Wednesday night, eight of the rescued whales have been returned to the ocean, and the last one, in poor health, continued to receive observation and full treatment. The bodies of another three dead whales were placed in frozen storage and will be used for research.

The whales were found stranded in a mudflat hundreds of meters from the shore in Linhai, Taizhou, East China's Zhejiang Province by local residents, who reported this to authorities at around 8 a.m. Tuesday. Local public security, fire, fishery and other departments and nearby enthusiastic fishermen quickly launched a rescue operation.

The rescue was extremely difficult due to the recent hot weather and the location, which was far from the shore, rescuers said. "The whales are about 2 meters long and very heavy, so it is difficult to move them."

The entire process of rescuing the whales was broadcast live by the media, with millions of people watching as rescuers went down to the sea and then held the whales in place, pouring water on them.

After rescuers worked together to get the whales onto stretchers and move them to a dug-out puddle, another wave of rescuers continued to spray them with water and used wet towels to prevent the water from evaporating. The rescue brigade also brought in ice to cool the whales down.

"Seeing the police and the public come together to quickly complete the rescue for such large animals is really moving," a Taizhou resident surnamed Wang, who lives nearby, told the *Global Times*.

Although whale strandings occur frequently along the coast, it is relatively rare for 12 to be stranded at one time, Sun Quanhui, a scientist from the World Animal Protection organization, told the *Global Times*.

The cause of the stranding of the whales is unclear. "Common causes include predation into unfamiliar waters, changes in seawater tides, neurological diseases, and malfunctioning navigation systems. It is generally believed that artificial sonar and diseases are the primary causes of disruption to cetacean navigational capabilities," Sun noted.

Sun pointed out that wild whales will find it difficult to adapt to captivity and should be released back into the sea as soon as possible after treatment of their injuries and illnesses, which was also the strategy of the rescue team on site.

Sun also expressed concern toward the whales' overall status. "The success rate of rescuing stranded cetaceans is often not high. Some sick or injured individuals may die during the rescue process, and some individual animals sometimes strand again even after returning to deep water."

Earlier this week, another rare whale was seen in the waters around Dapeng Bay in Shenzhen, South China's Guangdong Province. The Bryde's Whale, listed as a first-class national protected animal, was spotted on June 29 and has been staying in the area since then, according to the general office of Dapeng New District in Shenzhen.

Local officials established a special work team to protect the animal and called for boats to pass by without watching, which gained a lot of praise from netizens.

These successive appearances of whales in China's waters may indicate a change in the survival environment of cetaceans, experts noted.

"The Bryde's Whale has been staying for many days in Shenzhen waters and its obvious foraging behavior has been observed, indicating that the food resources in the waters are relatively abundant and the marine environment may be more suitable for the survival of marine mammals such as Bryde's Whales," Sun told the *Global Times*.

Due to overfishing, offshore pollution and busy shipping lanes, the survival of some cetaceans active in China's offshore waters used to be greatly affected, and many species were included in the recently updated *National List of Key Protected Wildlife*.

In addition to rescuing stranded whales in a timely manner, marine ecological protection should be enhanced comprehensively, Sun suggested, including increasing the number of marine protected areas and strictly implementing the policy of a marine fishing moratorium.

China's fishery authority began to carry out fishing moratoriums for Chinese fishermen on some part of high seas to conserve squid resources starting from July 1. From July 1 to September 30, the moratorium will be carried out in parts of the high seas of the southwest Atlantic Ocean outside the exclusive economic zones of relevant countries. From September 1 to November 30, the moratorium will be rolled out in parts of the high seas in the Eastern Pacific Ocean.

Words and Expressions

1. **strand:** to leave or drive (ships, fish, etc.) aground or ashore or (of ships, fish, etc.) to be left or driven ashore 搁浅

2. **evaporate:** If a liquid evaporates or if sth. evaporates it, it changes into a gas, especially steam. 蒸发

3. **predation:** the act of an animal killing and eating other animals 掠食

4. **neurological:** relating to nerves or to the science of neurology 神经系统的

5. **navigation:** the skill or the process of planning a route for a ship or vehicle and taking it there 领航；导航

6. **cetacean:** connected with the group of creatures that includes whales and dolphins 鲸目的；鲸类动物

7. **moratorium:** a temporary stopping of an activity, especially by official agreement 暂停

8. **fishery department** 渔政部门

Cultural Notes

1. **melon-headed whale:** It belongs to the oceanic dolphin family. It is closely related to the Pygmy killer whale and Pilot whale. Collectively these dolphin species are known by the common name "blackfish". Melon-headed whales have a rounded cone head which gives the animal its common name. The color of the body is light grey except for a dark grey face—sometimes called the "mask". The flippers are long and pointed. The dorsal fin is tall with a pointed tip. 瓜头鲸

2. **World Animal Protection organization:** It is an international non-profit animal welfare organization that has been in operation for over 30 years. The charity describes its mission as creating a better world for animals from the frontlines of disaster zones to the boardrooms of large corporations. 世界动物保护协会

3. **Bryde's Whale:** Bryde's Whales are also known as "tropical whales", due to their apparent preference for waters above 16° Celcius and concentration in latitudes between 40° south and 40° north. Although some seasonal movement between warmer and colder waters has been documented for some populations, others have been observed to reside year-round in coastal tropical or sub-tropical waters. They can be found both inshore and offshore, and tend to be associated with areas of high productivity, such as upwelling areas. 布氏鲸

4. ***National List of Key Protected Wildlife:*** China's *National List of Key Protected Wildlife* includes a total of 988 species of wildlife animals. The list was released in January 1989 and a major amendment was made to it in February 2021.《国家重点保护野生动物名录》

5. *The Global Times:* It is a daily tabloid newspaper under the auspices of *People's Daily* newspaper, commenting on international issues from a nationalistic perspective.《环球时报》

Exercises

I True or False

Read the text and make a judgment of the following statements.

1. All of the stranded whales have been rescued and returned to the ocean.
2. The rescue was extremely difficult due to the hot weather and the location.
3. The cause of the stranding of the whales is their malfunctioning navigation systems.
4. The stranded melon-headed whales have been the only appearance of whales found in China's waters in recent years.
5. Fishing moratoriums have been carried out for Chinese fishermen on some part of high seas to conserve squid resources.

II Reading Comprehension

Read the text and then answer the following questions.

1. What are the parties engaged in the rescue endeavor for the stranded whales?
2. How did the rescuers help the stranded whales before returning them to the sea?
3. What are the common causes of whale stranding?
4. What was the strategy of the rescue team on site for stranded whales?
5. Why did the survival of some cetaceans active in China's offshore waters use to be greatly affected?

III Discussion

Discuss the following questions based on the text.

1. What is the role of the live video broadcast in the rescue endeavor for the stranded whales?
2. What are the changes of marine ecosystem key to the reappearance of rare whales in China's waters?

IV Writing

Write an essay according to the following directions.

Animal performances in zoos and aquariums have received a lot of criticism in recent years and some argue that it is particularly immoral and cruel to keep large intelligent sea creatures like whales and dolphins confined to aquariums. What is your opinion on this? How do you think this controversy could be settled? Write an essay in no less than 250 words.

V Translation

Translate the following passage from English to Chinese.

In addition to rescuing stranded whales in a timely manner, marine ecological protection should be enhanced comprehensively, Sun suggested, including increasing the number of marine protected areas and strictly implementing the policy of a marine fishing moratorium. China's fishery authority began to carry out fishing moratoriums for Chinese fishermen on some part of high seas to conserve squid resources starting from July 1. From July 1 to September 30, the moratorium will be carried out in parts of the high seas of the southwest Atlantic Ocean outside the exclusive economic zones of relevant countries. From September 1 to November 30, the moratorium will be rolled out in parts of the high seas in the Eastern Pacific Ocean.

VI Project

Overfishing, offshore pollution and busy shipping lanes had been the main reasons that the survival of some cetaceans in China's offshore waters was affected. What specific measures have been taken by the Chinese government to ensure a better marine ecosystem for the cetaceans? Are there any other factors endangering the survival of cetaceans? Work in groups to find out the answers to these questions and present your findings in class.

Text B

Elephants' 500 km-Trek Across China Baffles Scientists

By Suranjana Tewari

Elephants are by nature fiercely intelligent beasts and experts who study them day in day out already know a great deal about them. And yet a herd of endangered elephants in China has completely dumbfounded scientists globally, while captivating an entire nation in the process.

It's not unusual for elephants to move small distances. But this herd has been lumbering its way across China for more than a year now. The elephants have now strayed almost 500 km (310 miles), a mammoth trek from their original habitat.

It's thought that they started their journey last spring from Xishuangbanna National Nature Reserve in the southwest of the country, near the border with Myanmar and Laos. They began moving north and in the last few months, the elephants have popped up in a number of villages, towns and cities.

They've been seen smashing down doors, raiding shops, "stealing" food, playing around in the mud, taking a bath in a canal and napping in the middle of a forest. They've also been spotted hoovering up crops in their wake and moseying into people's houses—on one occasion, lining up in a courtyard to drink water, successfully turning on a tap with their trunks.

It is thought they have started to move south again, and were last spotted in Shijie—a town near the city of Yuxi. It's unclear whether they are headed back, or why they even embarked on this journey in the first place—the farthest known movement by elephants in the country. Or what might come next.

Scientists Baffled

"The truth is, no one knows. It is almost certainly related to the need for resources—food, water, shelter—and this would make sense given the fact that in most locations where Asian elephants live in the wild, there is an increase in human disturbances leading to habitat fragmentation, loss and resource reduction," Joshua Plotnik, assistant professor of elephant psychology at Hunter College, City University of New York, told the BBC.

Mr. Plotnik added that the movement might have something to do with the social dynamics of the group. Elephants are matriarchal with the oldest and wisest female leading

the group of grandmothers, mothers and aunties along with their sons and daughters. After puberty, males break off and travel alone or link up in groups with other males for a short time. They only congregate with females temporarily to mate before leaving again.

However, this herd set out as a group of 16 or 17 elephants, including three males. Two males peeled off a month later, with one male moving away from the group earlier this month.

"It's not unusual, but I'm surprised he stayed that long. It was probably because of unfamiliar territory. When I saw them walking into a town or village, they were moving closely together—that's a sign of stress," said Ahimsa Campos-Arceiz, professor and principal investigator at the Xishuangbanna Tropical Botanical Garden.

Elephants are closer in behaviour to humans than other mammals, experiencing a range of emotions like joy in birth, grief in death and anxiety in unfamiliar territory.

Researchers were also taken by surprise when two of the female elephants gave birth on the journey." Elephants are very habitual and very routine-driven; it's unusual for them to move to new areas when they're about to give birth—they try to find the safest place they can," Lisa Olivier at Game Rangers International, a wildlife conservation organisation based in Zambia, told the BBC.

Ms. Olivier says the famous pictures of the elephants sleeping together are unusual too." Normally the babies are sleeping on the ground and the big ones lean against a tree or a termite mound. Because they're so big, that if there is any sort of threat it takes too long for them to get up and lying down puts a lot of pressure on their heart and lungs," she said.

"The fact that they were lying down suggests that they were all exhausted—totally wiped out—it all must be so new to them. So much of their communication is infrasonic sound—the vibration of their feet—but in the towns and cities they are hearing the sounds of vehicles."

Running out of Space

Scientists are unanimous that this is not migration because it does not follow a fixed route.

However, China is one of the few places in the world where the elephant population is growing thanks to extensive conservation efforts. China has cracked down hard on poaching and, as a result, the wild elephant population in Yunnan Province has gone from 193 in the 1990s to about 300 today.

But urbanisation and deforestation have reduced habitats for elephants and so, say experts, they could be looking for a new home with better access to food.

These giants of the jungle are mean eating machines, slaves to their gut, and so spend much of their lives looking for the 150 to 200 kg of food they need every day.

Watched from the Air

Experts are pleased the journey hasn't caused any dangerous confrontations with humans, and there are other positives.

The drones that authorities have deployed to monitor the elephants have given researchers a huge amount of quality information without disturbing the animals and provided an excited public with unforgettable photographs.

Ms. Olivier also highlights the cooperation between government, local authorities and conservation projects to protect the herd. In recent months, officials have been laying food bait and blocking roads with trucks to redirect the elephants to safety.

"I'm pleased that the approach is not very intrusive. A very common mistake is trying to tell elephants what they should be doing. Elephants aren't evolved to be told what to do. When we try to tell them what to do over long distances, it can create lots of aggressive behaviours," Mr. Campos-Arceiz said.

Chinese media have been checking in on the group of elephants daily. And the herd has become a social media hit with Internet users. All the attention has increased awareness and sensitivity to the plight of the endangered elephants in the country, and the global interest is likely to have far-reaching effects. "This attention and exposure will help conservation all over the world," according to Ms. Olivier.

Words and Expressions

1. **lumber:** to move in a slow, heavy and awkward way 缓慢而吃力地移动
2. **stray:** to wander away from where one is supposed to be 走失
3. **mammoth:** extremely large 巨大的
4. **hoover up:** to get or collect sth. in large quantities 获得大量的（某物）
5. **matriarchal:** controlled by women rather than men; passing power, property, etc. from mother to daughter rather than from father to son 母系的；女家长的
6. **congregate:** to come together in a group 聚集；群集
7. **mammal:** animals such as humans, dogs, lions, and whales 哺乳动物
8. **termite:** small insects that do a lot of damage by eating wood 白蚁
9. **wiped-out:** extremely tired 筋疲力尽的
10. **infrasonic:** having or relating to a frequency below the audibility range of the human ear 次声的

11. **crack down:** to take positive regulatory or disciplinary action 打击；制裁

12. **poach:** to illegally hunt birds, animals or fish 偷猎

13. **drone:** an aircraft without a pilot 无人机

14. **intrusive:** disturbing or annoying 侵入的；烦扰的

 ## Cultural Notes

1. **Xishuangbanna National Nature Reserve:** It lies in the counties of Jinghong, Mengla and Menghai, south of Yunnan Province. The Reserve covers a total area of 241,000 hectares, with its natural forest covering an area of 197,800 hectares and accounting for 81.8% of the total. Established in 1958, Xishuangbanna National Nature Reserve was accepted by UNESCO as a member of the International Man and Biosphere Reserve Network in 1993. Its main targets for protection are the tropical forest ecosystem, including marvelous virgin forests, tropical rain forest and monsoon rain forest as well as precious flora and fauna. It is also a safe, congenial habitat with ample food resources for a myriad of animals. 西双版纳国家自然保护区

2. **Xishuangbanna Tropical Botanical Garden:** Xishuangbanna Tropical Botanical Garden (XTBG) of Chinese Academy of Sciences (CAS) was founded under the leadership of the late eminent botanist Cai Xitao in 1959. Geographically, it lies between 101°25′E，21°41′N, with an elevation of 570 m above sea level. Its average annual temperature is 21.4℃. Following its separation from Kunming Institute of Botany and its combination with Kunming Institute of Ecology, the new XTBG came into being in 1997. It is a comprehensive research institution engaged in scientific research, species preservation, science communication, science & technology development, and a well-known scenic spot as well. 中国科学院西双版纳热带植物园

3. **Game Rangers International:** It is a Zambian conservation non-governmental organization established in 2008. It was founded with the specific aim of assisting the wildlife authorities and communities in the Kafue National Park area to better protect its valuable resource and environment. With a focus on the flagship African Elephant species, GRI currently implements five projects that together take a holistic approach to the problems of conservation and development, rooted in the belief that the key to sustainable, long-term utilisation of Zambia's natural wealth is best achieved by ensuring the full participation of its citizens in managing these vital, internationally important ecosystems. 巡护员国际

Exercises

❶ True or False

Read the text and make a judgment of the following statements.

1. Elephants are usually considered animals of low intelligence.
2. Scientists and experts are not certain why those elephants began their 500 km-trek journey.
3. A herd of elephants is usually led by the oldest and wisest male of the group.
4. China is one of the few places in the world where elephants are thriving.
5. Some scientists believe that this could be a migration.

❷ Reading Comprehension

Read the text and then answer the following questions.

1. Where and when do scientists believe the group of elephants started to move across China?
2. What is the common social dynamics of an elephant group?
3. Why were researchers surprised when two of the female elephants gave birth on the journey?
4. Why is it unusual for elephants to lie down when they are sleeping?
5. Why is it a wrong way to intrusively approach the strayed elephants?

❸ Discussion

Discuss the following questions based on the text.

1. Why do you think the journeying elephants captivated the entire nation's attention and became a hit on the Internet?
2. What did government and local authorities do to ensure the thriving of elephants in Yunnan Province?

❹ Writing

Write an essay according to the following directions.

The attention on the journeying elephants has increased awareness and sensitivity to the endangered giant creature. It seems that frequent exposure and good publicity could contribute to the betterment of wild animals, while it is also noted in the text that an intrusive approach is not desirable. What is your opinion on this? Write an essay in no less than 250 words.

V Translation

Translate the following passage from English to Chinese.

Scientists are unanimous that this is not migration because it does not follow a fixed route. However, China is one of the few places in the world where the elephant population is growing thanks to extensive conservation efforts. China has cracked down hard on poaching and, as a result, the wild elephant population in Yunnan Province has gone from 193 in the 1990s to about 300 today. But urbanisation and deforestation have reduced habitats for elephants and so, say experts, they could be looking for a new home with better access to food.

VI Project

What do you think are most likely to be the reasons that the elephants started their journey and why? Work in groups to conduct your own research and present your conclusion in class.

Text C

Biodiversity Conservation in China Has Improved but More Efforts Are Needed

By Wan Lin

China's biodiversity conservation and environment protection awareness has been growing thanks to increased government investment and local online crowd funding. However, more realistic actions are needed from officials and the public, said a frontline conservationist and protector of the endangered gibbon in China.

Yan Lu, cofounder of Cloud Mountain Conservation, shared her views with the *Global Times* ahead of the celebration of the International Day for Biological Diversity on Saturday. The Cloud Mountain Conservation is a non-governmental organization (NGO) dedicated to the protection of gibbons in China. With less than 1,500 left across the country, wild gibbons are fewer than giant pandas.

The organization gained the public's attention after Fan Pengfei, cofounder of the NGO and professor at Sun Yat-sen University, discovered a new species of gibbon in Southwest China's Yunnan Province in 2017, which he named the Skywalker hoolock gibbon.

A frontline conservationist and operator of an NGO for one of China's most threatened creatures, Yan has personally experienced the changes in the country's biodiversity conservation awareness over the years.

"The growth of online crowd funding platforms and an increasingly stronger funding from tens of millions of Chinese netizens have provided growing financial support to us and other grass-roots level NGOs that joined our cause to protect wildlife," she said.

Sina Weibo, WeChat and Alipay are the main platforms where conservationists and the general public can donate money to Cloud Mountain Conservation, she said, adding that the resources collected from crowd funding can be more than half of the total annual income of the organization.

Song Dazhao, founder of the Chinese Felid Conservation Alliance, shared the same experience. He told the *Global Times* on Sunday that the organization has seen a growing proportion of online crowd funding in its total income over the years, reaching nearly 50 percent.

The introduction of a series of reforms and policies by the government in recent years has also changed China's status in the protection of the environment and conservation of the biodiversity, according to Yan.

"The new policies and measures the government introduced for wildlife protection, such as setting ecological thresholds, have provided guidelines for officials from different organs to implement biodiversity conservation guidelines. These actions indeed showed the determination of the government," she said.

China is the third-most biodiverse country in the world with over 34,000 unclassified species of animals and plants, according to International Union for Conservation of Nature (IUCN).

However, it is also among the countries with the most threatened species, with more than 1,000 known species in the country that are categorized as critically endangered, endangered, or vulnerable, according to the IUCN.

To enhance the national efforts in protecting biodiversity, China issued a reform plan in 2015 to increase accountability for officials at all levels and in different fields, and established the National Committee on Biodiversity Conservation in December 2020 to strengthen the departmental coordination and linkage from top to bottom.

The country has effectively protected 90 percent of plants and terrestrial ecosystems, 65 percent of higher plant communities and 85 percent of key wildlife populations over the past 40 years since its accession to the Convention on International Trade in Endangered Species of Wild Fauna and Flora, according to Zhang Zhizhong, Director of the wildlife protection department of China's State Forestry and Grassland Administration.

The population of rare and endangered species of animals and plants, such as the giant panda, the crested ibis, and cycas and dove trees, have been recovering and growing, he said.

Although much progress has been made in China's environmental protection, the lack of public awareness about endangered species and environmental protection, as well as the absence of concrete actions from government officials, remain the main obstacles for China to join the team of developed countries that champion biodiversity conservation, Yan noted.

"Surely it is hard to see a big change within a short time, the government can at least gradually increase the priority level of wildlife protection in their overall work plan and try to have a deep understanding of the relevant policies before implementing them," she said.

Song told the *Global Times* that the only problem for China's biodiversity conservation lies on how to take concrete actions, even though the investment and attention made by the government and the public has improved to a large extent compared with 10 years ago.

China will hold for the first time the 15th meeting of the Conference of the Parties to the Convention on Biological Diversity (COP15) in October in Kunming, Yunnan Province, one of the cities with most biodiversity in the country.

Both conservationists said they have been actively preparing for the conference, along with many other Chinese local NGOs, under the guidance of the Ministry of Ecology and Environment and relevant foundations.

"It is a very important achievement for our country to get the right to host the COP15 at the current time," said Yan, noting that Cloud Mountain Conservation will present a few cases of their project on endangered gibbons in China.

Despite being one of the first countries to join the Convention on Biological Diversity, China's actions and progress in wildlife protection and biodiversity conservation have long been neglected and sometimes even misunderstood by the world. Therefore the COP15 is a good opportunity for the Chinese government and NGOs to showcase the achievements gained today, she said.

Unit 4

Chinese Food

导读

　　随着纪录片《舌尖上的中国》的播出，源远流长的中国饮食文化再一次成为热点话题。除了丰富可口的美食本身，承载美食的人物故事和风土人情也成为人们关注的焦点。该纪录片在国内风靡的同时，还引发了海外的关注。《卫报》对《舌尖上的中国》的盛赞展现了外国人眼中的中国美食和饮食文化；BBC则从风土、习俗、历史等不同角度解读了中国古话"民以食为天"。

Text A

A Bite of China: The Finest Food TV Ever?

By Oliver Thring

Every autumn, the Yangtze River in Hubei Province, begins to drop and the nearby lakes become thick bogs covered in webs of detritus. Men come in little boats, perhaps 100 a day, paddling their way across the sinking river in the dim, blue-grey light before sunrise. They're looking for lotus root, the starchy staple that is a highlight of much Asian cooking, and gives a sweetish solidity to a winter soup.

I'd never given a thought to where lotus root comes from. Getting hold of it turns out to be fantastically difficult, dirty and dangerous. The roots, perhaps a metre or two long, lie deep in the thick, gluey mud of the lake bed. They're fragile, and snap or scratch easily, and there's no machinery to get them out. You wade out into the bog, the mud coming up to your knees, and find a root, work out which direction it's lying in, then dig it out slowly and carefully by hand. At the end of another 14-hour day, the workers compare their aches, torn muscles, sprained ankles and twisted ligaments like soldiers or a rugby team. They hope for particularly nasty winters, which mean that more people make lotus-root soup, and the price of their product rises.

This is just one segment of the best TV show I've ever seen about food. I'd hazard it's the best one ever made. *A Bite of China* began airing in May on the state broadcaster there. Thirty of the country's most respected filmmakers worked for more than a year filming the seven 50-minute episodes. They shot throughout the country, from the frozen lakes of the northeast to the bamboo forests of Liuzhou.

As always, the people are the most interesting part: An old woman looking for matsutake mushrooms on pathless mountainsides, a family making kimchi in the Kingan mountains, a fisherman catching barracuda for his supper, a Shanghai woman filling her bathtub with live crabs to make drunken crab, drowning the creatures in wine and storing them in earthenware. But though the programme explains that the lives of many of its subjects are difficult and that the people are poor, it stunningly captures ways of life that are evaporating in modern China.

Each episode adopts a theme: preserving by salt, pickling or wind, staple foods, the "gifts of nature" or "our rural heritage". The filmmakers explore the central idea using examples from across the country. Perspective shifts from the macro—helicopter shots of neon cities or canopied mountains rearing out of lakes—to the micro—a single bamboo shoot pushing through the earth.

There are plans to screen *A Bite of China* in 20 countries including Germany and the USA, but the show is only available on YouTube at the moment. The amateur translation can be a bit ropey. (Elderly people enjoying food: "Even though their tastebuds are in degeneration phase, they still remember their hometown deliciousness.")

But what I love most about the programme is that it never patronises its subjects or viewers. It takes for granted the fact that what it has to show is worth watching, and devotes itself to making the final cut look as ravishing as possible. It's not, strictly speaking, a cookery programme, though we see a lot of people cooking and there's a recipe book tie-in (currently available only in Chinese). Instead it's educational in a more traditional, Reithian sense. It's perhaps the food TV equivalent of *The Ascent of Man* or Lord Clark's *Civilisation* or the best of Attenborough.

British food TV has had its moments, but has never attempted anything like this. And it's impossible, having watched a couple of episodes of *A Bite of China*, not to feel a little humbled or even ashamed when you turn to your own country's food TV output and find Sophie Dahl and the Hairy Bikers.

Words and Expressions

1. **detritus:** natural waster material that is left after sth. has been used or broken up 风化物；腐殖质
2. **paddle:** to move through water using a short pole with a wide flat part at one end or at both ends 划桨
3. **lotus:** a tropical plant with white or pink flower that grows on the surface of lakes in Africa and Asia 莲
4. **starchy:** containing a lot of starch 富含淀粉的
5. **sprain:** to injure a joint by a sudden twisting or bending 扭伤
6. **ligament:** a band of strong tissue in a person's body which connects bones 韧带
7. **matsutake:** a large brownish edible mushroom having film flesh and a spicy aroma 松茸
8. **kimchi:** a vegetable pickle seasoned with garlic, red pepper and ginger that is the national dish of Korea 韩国泡菜
9. **barracuda:** a large tropical sea fish that eats other fish 梭鱼
10. **earthenware:** pottery 陶器

11. **neon:** Neon lights are made from glass tubes filled with neon gas which produce a bright electric light 霓虹的

12. **canopied:** covered with a roof or a piece of material supported by poles 有顶棚的；有华盖的

13. **ropey:** inferior or inadequate 劣质的；不足的

14. **degeneration:** the process of becoming worse or less acceptable in quality or condition 蜕化；衰退

15. **patronize:** to treat someone in a way that seems friendly, but which shows that you think they are not very intelligent, or that they are inferior to you, etc. 屈尊俯就地对待

16. **ravishing:** extremely beautiful 引人入胜的；令人陶醉的

 ## Cultural Notes

1. **Reithian:** of, relating to, or characteristic of John, 1st Baron Reith, the British public servant and first director general of the BBC. It is especially related to his principles regarding the responsibility of broadcasting to enlighten and educate the public. BBC 第一任总裁约翰·里斯式的（价值观等）

2. *The Ascent of Man:* The first episode of *The Ascent of Man* was broadcast on 5 May, 1973. The 13-part series, written and presented by Jacob Bronowski—was one of the landmarks of documentary television. It was presented as a personal view of humanity's scientific achievement, exploring science, as *Civilisation* had explored art. Both series were commissioned by David Attenborough, Controller of BBC2, who later presented his own landmark series, *Life on Earth*.《人类的攀升》

3. *Civilisation: Civilisation*—in full, *Civilisation: A Personal View* by Kenneth Clark—is a television documentary series written and presented by the art historian Kenneth Clark. The thirteen programmes in the series outline the history of Western art, architecture and philosophy since the Dark Ages. The series was produced by the BBC and aired in 1969 on BBC2. And in later transmissions in Britain, the US and other countries, it reached an unprecedented number of viewers for an art series.《文明》

4. **Attenbough:** Sir David Frederick Attenborough is an English broadcaster and natural historian. He is best known for writing and presenting, in conjunction with the BBC Natural History Unit, the nine natural history documentary series forming the *Life* collection that together constitute a comprehensive survey of animal and plant life on Earth. He is a former senior manager at the BBC, having served as controller of BBC2 and director of programming for BBC Television in the 1960s and 1970s. He is the only person to have won BAFTAs for programmes in each of black and white, colour, HD, 3D and 4K. 大卫·爱登堡

Unit 4 Chinese Food

5. **Sophie Dahl:** Sophie Dahl grew up in the midst of a greedy extended family, whose members all loved to cook and eat. She began her working life as a fashion model, but writing was always her first love. In 2003, her first book, an illustrated novella called *The Man with the Dancing Eyes*, was published. This was followed by a novel, *Playing with the Grown-ups*. A devoted home-cook, Dahl wrote her cookbook *Miss Dahl's Voluptuous Delights* in 2009. A BBC2 series, *The Delicious Miss Dahl*, based on some of the recipes and stories from the book, aired the following year. In 2011 she wrote and presented a BBC2 social history documentary about the Victorian domestic advisor Isabella Beeton, shortly after her second cookbook, *From Season to Season*, was published. 苏菲·达儿

6. **The Hairy Bikers:** The Hairy Bikers are David Myers and Simon King, two northern blokes with a passion for cooking and food. The pair began their TV careers working behind the scenes, Simon as a first assistant director and locations manager for film and television and David as a BBC make-up artist specialising in prosthetics. It was on the set of a TV drama that they first met and became friends. The cooks first appeared in front of the camera for their pilot *Hairy Bikers* series, filmed in Portugal. No strangers to travel before they started working together, the lads embraced the opportunity to seek out new dishes from around the globe when their show took off. 毛毛骑手

Exercises

I True or False

Read the text and make a judgment of the following statements.

1. The process of collecting lotus roots is considered by the author as hard, unhygienic and risky.
2. All the episodes of *A Bite of China* share a common theme.
3. There is no plan to broadcast *A Bite of China* anywhere outside China.
4. According to the author, there is no patronization in *A Bite of China*.
5. The author believes that *A Bite of China* is more attempting than any other British food TV.

II Reading Comprehension

Read the text and then answer the following questions.

1. How are lotus roots usually collected?
2. What else does *A Bite of China* capture beside the various Chinese people it covers?
3. What are the themes of the episodes of *A Bite of China*?
4. How does the filmmaker explore and demonstrate the themes?
5. What does the author love most about *A Bite of China*?

Ⅲ Discussion

Discuss the following questions based on the text.

1. How do you like *A Bite of China*? What is the most appealing about this TV show? What is your favorite episode or shot?
2. *A Bite of China* has been very popular domestically and internationally. What do you think is its recipe for success?

Ⅳ Writing

Write an essay according to the following directions.

A Bite of China demonstrates the history of Chinese food, eating and cooking in various ways. The voiceover in the TV show is just as expressive as the pictures and videos. If you are to introduce a traditional food from your hometown and its culinary culture, how would you do it? Write an essay in no less than 250 words.

Ⅴ Translation

Translate the following passage from English to Chinese.

As always, the people are the most interesting part: An old woman looking for matsutake mushrooms on pathless mountainsides, a family making kimchi in the Kingan mountains, a fisherman catching barracuda for his supper, a Shanghai woman filling her bathtub with live crabs to make drunken crab, drowning the creatures in wine and storing them in earthenware. But though the programme explains that the lives of many of its subjects are difficult and that the people are poor, it stunningly captures ways of life that are evaporating in modern China.

Ⅵ Project

According to the author, *A Bite of China* captures the ways of life that are evaporating in China. What are those lifestyles? Why do you think they are evaporating? How can we preserve them? Watch the episodes and work in groups to find out about them. Then present your findings in class.

Text B

To the People, Food Is Heaven

By BBC Storyworks

China is the home of 1.4 billion foodies. That might seem like hyperbole, but in the world's most populous country, food culture is simply just culture. The art of cultivating, cooking and eating food is profoundly interwoven with what it means to be Chinese, whether you're a farmer, factory worker or tech billionaire. In China, the phrase "Have you eaten?" is how friends and neighbours greet one another. Food is business, pleasure, health and happiness. Food is life. It's the glue that binds all Chinese people together, regardless of background, social circle or bank balance.

Food Is Adventure

China is undeniably vast, encompassing mighty mountain ranges and rivers, rainforests, grassland, deserts and coast. When the sun sets on the eastern edge of the Great Wall, it takes almost two hours until it dips behind its far-western reaches along the old Silk Road into Central Asia. When rice farmers in straw hats sow their seeds in southern regions such as Guizhou Province, thousands of kilometres to the north in icy Heilongjiang, fur-clad fishermen are cutting holes in ice to net their catch.

China's incredible diversity of climate and terrain, upon which civilisation has flourished for thousands of years, equals a seemingly endless spread of cuisines and dishes. Journey south to Guangdong Province and you'll encounter the tradition of breakfast dim sum served from creaky carts piled high with *shaomai* dumplings, steamers of "phoenix claws" (aka chicken feet), sweet custard tarts and other delicate treats, all washed down with copious cups of tea.

Over in China's Sichuan Basin, everything from noodles to tofu to bullfrog are served up with a one-two punch—the marriage of chilli heat with the mouth-numbing tickle of Sichuan peppercorns. In coastal Qingdao, heaps of stir-fried clams are washed down with the city's famous beer. In arid Gansu Province, Hui Muslim chefs twirl bunched ribbons of chewy wheat noodles before serving them in beef broth, while in far-flung Yunnan Province, jutting up against Laos, Vietnam and Myanmar, you could slurp fragrant rice noodles for every meal and nobody would raise an eyebrow.

Food Is Celebration

In China, where feasting is a way of life, the table is so often the setting for life's many

milestones and memorable occasions. Every Chinese New Year, the world's largest human migration takes place, as millions make the journey home to celebrate with loved ones. For many working families scattered like seeds across the country, it's the one annual occasion when they all come together, which makes the "Reunion Dinner" on Chinese New Year's Eve one of the most cherished meals of the year. The feast typically features auspicious dishes aplenty, including fish which sounds like the word for "surplus"; and dumplings, prepared and wrapped communally, which promise wealth and good fortune by their resemblance to old silver ingots.

Most meals throughout the year in China are served family-style, where communal dishes are shared between diners. Eating this way is an expression of community and togetherness, even when just partaken by a few friends, classmates or colleagues. The joy of shared dining is best embodied in interactive food experiences such as huoguo, (hotpot), where diners cook their own food by scalding raw meat, vegetables, tofu and other ingredients in a bubbling cauldron of soup. These can be wickedly spicy, such as Chongqing's famous sweat fest, or more austere such as Beijing-style shuan yang rou, where slices of hand-cut lamb are cooked in a clear broth then dunked in sesame sauce before eating.

Food Is History

Many famous Chinese dishes have a profound link to the past. In the 14th century, Peking duck was an imperial dish, the food of emperors. It's likely that the recipe found its way into well-heeled residences and restaurants. Some of these would become household brands known as "laozihao" (time-honored brands). Bianyifang, a famous Peking duck "laozihao" with branches throughout the capital, was established in 1416. Quanjude, another "laozihao" established four centuries later, pioneered the technique of roasting ducks by hanging them in open ovens over the wood of fruit trees to impart aromatic flavour into the meat and wrapping the meat in thin wheat pancakes.

Historically, food has also been inseparable from Chinese medicine and health. During the Tang Dynasty (618–907), many texts were produced about the Tao of eating, covering diet, nutrition and food therapy. Then, as now, the Chinese believe that the way to holistic health and wellbeing is through your stomach.

Food Is Diversity

Universal use of chopsticks and seasonings such as soy sauce has fuelled the misconception outside China that its cuisine is homogenous. In fact, China's patchwork of food regions is similar in size and has a diversity of taste and techniques approaching that of the countries of Europe. In the wheat belt of the dry, colder north, dense breads, chewy noodles and dumplings dominate, along with stewed meats and preserved foods. A love of yoghurt in the north comes courtesy of the pastoral Mongolians and Manchu peoples formerly of the grasslands beyond the Great Wall. In the far west on the Himalayan Plateau, Tibetan cuisine is based around tsampa (a staple of roasted barley flour) and milk tea enriched with yak-butter.

In contrast, China's well-watered southern climes are dominated by rice, a huge abundance of produce and seafood, and an obsession with fresh ingredients and culinary perfection. Huaiyang cuisine, in the lower reaches of the Yangtze, is as artistic and sophisticated as the sculpted gardens of Suzhou. In once-remote regions such as Yunnan Province, home to dozens of distinct ethnic groups, locals dish up everything from edible flowers to rare mountain mushrooms; even fried goat cheese. Historically, Chinese food is subdivided into the "Eight Great Cuisines", but in practice, the regional differences can be broken down much further. Every place—even small towns—are famed for certain produce, from walnuts to watermelons. Some places are attached to a signature dish, such as the soup dumplings of Shanghai, or jingde chicken in Jingdezhen, birthplace of Chinese porcelain.

Food Is Heaven

A well-known Chinese epithet goes: "To the people, food is heaven". Even though the line comes from an ancient text written about 2,000 years ago in the Han Dynasty, today it rings truer than ever. The speed of change over the past half-century in China has been breathless, but one thing that has remained constant is China's cultural connection with food. Even though a Chinese city today might look quite unrecognisable compared to how it once did, its unique food identity in the form of produce, provenance and dishes remains as robust as ever. In fast-changing China, food is one of the most important anchors to a sense of cultural identity. A love, appreciation and understanding of food defines what it is to be Chinese, and no matter what happens in the future, that is never likely to change. Its cuisine may be available around the world, but to really appreciate its cultural significance, and sheer variety, you can't better experience it in its homeland.

Words and Expressions

1. **interweave:** to connect and combine closely with each other（使）交织；混杂
2. **encompass:** to include a large number or range of things 包含；涉及（大量事物）
3. **copious:** in large amount 大量的；充裕的
4. **auspicious:** showing signs that sth. is likely to be successful in the future 吉祥的
5. **ingot:** a lump of metal, usually shaped like a brick 铸块；锭
6. **scalding:** extremely hot（液体）滚烫的
7. **cauldron:** a large deep pot for boiling liquids or cooking food over a fire 大锅

8. **austere:** simple and plain 简单的；朴素的

9. **broth:** thick soup made by boiling meat or fish and vegetables in water 肉汤；鱼汤

10. **aromatic:** having a pleasant noticeable smell 芳香的

11. **holistic:** considering a whole thing or being to be more than a collection of parts 整体性的

12. **misconception:** an idea that is not correct 错误认识

13. **homogenous:** consisting of things or people that are all the same or all of the same type 同种类的

14. **walnut:** an edible nut that has a wrinkled shape and a hard round shell that is light brown in colour 胡桃

15. **provenance:** the place that sth. originally came from 起源

16. **robust:** strong and not likely to fail or become weak 强劲的；有活力的

17. **anchor:** a person or thing that gives sb. a feeling of safety 精神支柱

Cultural Notes

1. **dim sum:** It is a traditional Chinese meal made up of small plates of dumplings and other snack dishes and is usually accompanied by tea. Similar to the way that the Spanish eat tapas, the dishes are shared among family and friends. Typically, dim sum is consumed during brunch hours—late morning to lunchtime. The dishes are believed to have originated in the southern China's Guangdong region. Nowadays, dim sum can include dishes and traditions adopted from other parts of China. But by and large, the culinary form remains the same as ever.（广式）点心

2. **Chinese New Year's Eve:** Chinese New Year's Eve or Lunar New Year's Eve is the day before the Chinese New Year. Celebrating Chinese New Year's Eve has always been a family matter in China, because it is the reunion day for every Chinese family. It has evolved over a long period of time. The origin of Chinese New Year's Eve can be traced back to 3,500 years ago. Its practice is the cluster of this festival's history and tradition for thousands of years, and there are many practices in China which are varied as people in different regions have different customs. Most of the practices exists for thousands of years and are still being used nowadays. 除夕

3. **Bianyifang:** This "laozihao" (time-honored brand) restaurant, whose first branch is located in the historic Qianmen area, has been serving up some of the capital's finest duck since 1855. While Quanjudee is today the mightiest duck restaurant around, Bianyifang is said to have been the kingpin up until 1949. Whatever the history, Bianyifang's slow roast recipe undoubtedly yields mouthwatering results. 便宜坊

4. **Quanjude:** A name synonymous in Beijing with roast duck, Quanjude's celebrated birds have passed through the mouths of visitors from Fidel Castro to Richard Nixon over the

years. Watch your *kaoya* being sliced before your eyes, then roll slivers of duck—famed for the layer of juicy fat which lies under a crisp golden-brown skin—in pancakes with shallots and cucumber. Quanjude has venues in visitor hot spots all over town, from Wangfujing and the Silk Market to Shuangjing and the Qianmen branch. They continue to serve their birds by the tourist busload. 全聚德

5. **Eight Great Cuisines:** Chinese cuisine is rich and diverse, varying in style and taste from region to region. Its history dates back thousands of years, evolving according to changes in both the environment (such as climate) and local preferences over time. Chinese cuisine also varies depending on class and ethnic background, and it is often influenced by the cuisines of other cultures. All these factors contribute to an unparalleled range of cooking techniques, ingredients, dishes and eating styles that make up what is understood to be Chinese food today. The Eight Culinary Cuisines are Anhui, Cantonese, Fujian, Hunan, Jiangsu, Shandong, Sichuan and Zhejiang Cuisine. 八大菜系

Exercises

I True or False

Read the text and make a judgment of the following statements.

1. China enjoys an incredible diversity of climate and terrain.
2. Dim sum is Guangdong's traditional breakfast and is served in different dishes.
3. A typical "Reunion Dinner" usually includes fish because of its unique flavor.
4. In China, most of year communal dishes are shared by diners.
5. Peking duck had always been a dish for common people in ancient China.

II Reading Comprehension

Read the text and then answer the following questions.

1. What different kinds of terrain are encompassed by China?
2. What are the common dishes of dim sum?
3. What are the typical auspicious dishes of the "Reunion Dinner" and what do they stand for?
4. How is Chongqing hotpot different from Beijing-style *shuan yang rou*?
5. Why is there the misconception outside China that Chinese cuisine is homogenous?

Ⅲ Discussion

Discuss the following questions based on the text.

1. According to the text, Chinese food has been inseparable from Chinese medicine and health. How are they correlated? Can you give some examples?
2. How do you understand the Chinese epithet "To the people, food is heaven"?

Ⅳ Writing

Write an essay according to the following directions.

Chinese food and eating are quite different from those of the west. Communal dishes shared by diners is an example mentioned in the text. What about other differences in food, eating and cooking between China and the west? What cultural factors lead to those differences? Write an essay in no less than 250 words.

Ⅴ Translation

Translate the following passage from English to Chinese.

A well-known Chinese epithet goes: "To the people, food is heaven". Even though the line comes from an ancient text written about 2,000 years ago in the Han Dynasty, today it rings truer than ever. The speed of change over the past half-century in China has been breathless, but one thing that has remained constant is China's cultural connection with food. Even though a Chinese city today might look quite unrecognisable compared to how it once did, its unique food identity in the form of produce, provenance and dishes remains as robust as ever. In fast-changing China, food is one of the most important anchors to a sense of cultural identity. A love, appreciation and understanding of food defines what it is to be Chinese, and no matter what happens in the future, that is never likely to change. Its cuisine may be available around the world, but to really appreciate its cultural significance, and sheer variety, you can't better experience it in its homeland.

Ⅵ Project

There are Eight Great Cuisines in China, including Anhui, Cantonese, Fujian, Hunan, Jiangsu, Shandong, Sichuan and Zhejiang Cuisine. Which one is your favorite? Choose one of the eight cuisines and work in groups to find out more about its food, cooking and culture. Present your findings in class.

Text C

The Chinese Tea Ceremony: A Fascinating Ritual

By the editorial team of the blog "Laboratorio dell'Espresso"

Tea has always been an important part of Asian culture and particularly Chinese culture. Drinking it does not just mean consuming a drink; it means taking part in a real ritual, which has been preserved for many centuries keeping all its fascination intact. The traditional Chinese tea ceremony is often held during important occasions, such as weddings, but it is also a way to welcome guests into your home. Let's outline its history together and find out what it involves.

Tea in China

The history of Chinese tea starts around 5,000 years ago. Its consumption reached considerable levels during the Song Dynasty and grew throughout the Yuan Dynasty. At the beginning of the 16th century, the drink became widespread at all social levels, from the highest social ranks down to the less wealthy population.

Tea has always had a particularly important role in China, so much so that tribute is paid to the varieties produced in the areas considered to be the best. Indeed they are consumed at court, like the tea from Wuyi Mountain for example, subsequently known in the West as Bohea tea, whose fame and success originated in the Yuan Dynasty.

The History of the Chinese Tea Ceremony

One of the first written reports about this ceremony dates back to 1,200 years ago, during the Tang Dynasty. Behind the origins of this ceremony there is a religious idea in the form of a great respect for nature, linked to the philosophies of Confucianism, Taoism and Buddhism. Tea was first used in China for medicinal purposes, by the monks in the temples who used it for its phytotherapeutic benefits.

With the passing of time, the tea ceremony in China assumed a different connotation though, with a stronger sense of social occasion, becoming more a moment to spend together in harmony or a celebration of important life events. Of all the tea ceremonies, perhaps the most well-known is the one involving the preparation of Gongfu tea, which dates back to the 18th century. Widely used in recent years for tourist entertainment, this is the tea ceremony where the Oolong varieties of tea are prepared and served as a sign of respect for the guests.

The Wu-Wo tea ceremony, also quite popular, is a particularly spiritual ritual, which encourages the participants to forget their knowledge and wealth, to establish group equality, without any prejudice. In Chinese Buddhist usage, *wuwo*, which derives from Sanskrit, means "no individual independent existence". The Wu-Wo tea ceremony began in Taiwan, China, and extended to other regions all over the world.

What Utensils Are Needed for the Chinese Tea Ceremony?

First of all, during the ceremony everything must be perfect: from the attitude of those who take part to the atmosphere in which the ritual takes place, right down to the equipment used. In fact, some instruments are indispensable: First of all, a Chinese tea set, which can easily be bought online or in a specialist shop. The tea service is called *cha dao*, which means "the way of tea".

In general, a special Yixing teapot is used, but a porcelain one will do just as well. The jug, or *chahai* is used to guarantee the flavor of the tea. You will also need a tray, a canvas or small tray cloth (it is considered rude not to use one), a teaspoon or other suitable tools to clean the spout of the teapot.

Even the selection of the tea (strictly in leaf form) is fundamental: The Oolong varieties are those most widely used for the traditional ceremony. It is rarer, but the Pu-erh variety can also be used. For the Gongfu tea ceremony, green tea is usually avoided. The perfect tea should be prepared using the purest and cleanest water firstly to ensure that the drink has an impeccable taste, but also out of respect for nature itself. Even the technique must be impeccable: The tea must be served with relaxing and graceful movements.

The Moments of the Chinese Tea Ceremony

A well-organized ceremony lasts from 20 to 25 minutes and includes the following steps:

- First of all, you need to warm the teapot and the cups;
- Then, the tea is distributed to the participants, who look closely at the appearance, the smell and the quality;
- The third phase involves the actual preparation of the tea: You need to position the teapot on top of the bowl, lift the kettle up to shoulder height and pour the water into the teapot until it overflows. After pouring the water, the executor collects the leaves and puts them in the boiling water and puts the lid on the teapot;
- The following step is the brewing of the tea, which may vary according to the quantity of leaves, their quality and size. Usually, for Oolong tea, the brewing time ranges from 30 seconds to a maximum of 10 minutes. At this point, the guest pours the drink from the teapot into the tea pitcher. This is then poured into the glasses and transferred into the cups;

- The final step is the consumption. Good etiquette dictates that the drinkers should swing the cup gently using both hands to enjoy the aroma of the tea before tasting it. The drink should then be drunk in three sips. When everyone in the group has finished their first round of tea, then other rounds can be served.

Unit 5

Education in China

导读

  2020 年初，新冠病毒暴发，给中国社会带来了比较严重的影响。中国的学生因为疫情不能回到学校学习，只能在家上学。为了响应教育部"停课不停学"的号召，从小学到大学，神州大地开始了线上教学的新实验。很多一线教师变成了"网络主播"，师生都开启了线上学习的新模式。线上学习带给教师和学生怎样的体验？效果如何？我们拭目以待。中国的数学基础教育在世界上处于领先地位。国内外的教育专家和大众对于中国模式下的数学教育褒贬不一。上海数学教育模式因为学生在数学测试中的优异表现而引人关注，获得了国内外的认可。上海的数学教学方法有哪些特色，其他国家需要学习这种方法吗？让我们一起通过阅读来探索答案。

Text A

Getting to Know Your Teacher

By an anonymous author

"Don't delete your browser history," Lin Kai warns his 11-year-old son, who is supposed to be live-streaming lectures delivered by his schoolteachers. Mr. Lin has reason to be anxious. To curb the spread of COVID-19, the authorities have closed schools and universities indefinitely. But "study must not stop", says the Ministry of Education. Under its orders, the country's biggest exercise in remote learning is under way, watched over by parents. Mr. Lin, who lives in the eastern city of Hangzhou, has caught his son being distracted by online games. He wants his son to know that he will inspect the browser for evidence of such naughtiness.

There are other ways to enforce discipline. Liu Weihua, who teaches at Wuhan University of Technology, cold-calls his students during live streams. With sitdown exams now impossible, his grading system places more emphasis on how students perform in classroom discussions, Mr. Liu explains. These are conducted using video-conferencing platforms such as Dingtalk by Alibaba, a tech giant, and Ketang by Tencent, a competitor.

Slow Internet speeds at home are no excuse for shirking, says Yue Qiu, a secondary-school teacher in Beijing. If connections are too wobbly for video calls, students can download audio files and assignments. Parental supervision is encouraged. The municipal government of Beijing has decreed that, in households with two working parents, one is entitled to stay home without any loss of pay.

In poor rural areas, where some households lack Internet access, instruction by television fills the void. Since February 17th China Education Network, a state-run service, has been broadcasting classes every weekday from 8 a.m. to 10 p.m. The first lesson of the day is aimed at pupils in the first year of primary school. Programmes for older children air in the afternoon and evening. All core subjects, such as mathematics and Chinese, are covered.

The disruption is felt most keenly by pupils in the final year of secondary school. That is the year leading up to *gaokao*, the university-entrance exam. Many parents fret that online learning is a poor substitute for classroom instruction. Hou Kaixuan, who will sit *gaokao* in the northern city of Zhangjiakou this summer, eagerly awaits the re-opening of his school. "I'm simply more productive in a physical classroom," he says.

Not all his classmates agree. Kaixuan observes that some of them study just as hard at home as in school, and take perverse pleasure in the fact that others must be slacking off. (It helps that very little new material is taught in the last year of secondary school. The emphasis is on revision.)

When schools and universities eventually re-open, classrooms may be different, says Mr. Yue, the teacher in Beijing. The teacher-student relationship will become "less hierarchical", he predicts. That is because China's prolonged experiment with online learning is reducing the typical reserve between instructor and pupil. Teachers who were previously reluctant to give out their contact details on WeChat, a messaging app, now rely on it to respond to students' queries. At Mr. Yue's school, students may even call their teachers to ask for feedback. If he is right, such a breaking-down of barriers could be one of the few happy byproducts of the epidemic.

Words and Expressions

1. browser history 浏览历史
2. live-streaming 现场直播
3. remote learning 远程学习
4. **shirk:** to deliberately avoid doing something you should do, because you are lazy 逃避，逃课
5. **wobbly:** moving unsteadily from side to side 不太好的，不稳定的
6. physical classroom 实体课堂
7. slack off 懈怠
8. **hierarchical:** If a system, organization, etc. is hierarchical, people or things are divided into levels of importance. 按等级划分的；等级制度的
9. **byproduct:** something that is produced during the manufacture or processing of another product 副产品

Cultural Notes

1. **Wuhan University of Technology:** WUT was merged on May 27th 2000, from the former Wuhan University of Technology (established in 1948), Wuhan Transportation University (established in 1946) and Wuhan Automotive Polytechnic University (established in 1958). WUT is one of the leading Chinese universities under the direct administration of the Ministry of Education and one of the universities in the country's construction plan of world-class universities and first-class disciplines. 武汉理工大学

2. **Tencent:** a Chinese conglomerate founded in 1998 that specializes in technology, entertainment and AI worldwide. Tencent includes several subsidiaries and is known for its video games and WeChat social networking app. 腾讯

Exercises

I True or False

Read the text and make a judgment of the following statements.

1. Lin Kai warns his 11-year-old son to delete his browser history.
2. Liu Weihua, who teaches at Wuhan University of Technology, cold-calls his students during live streams to enforce discipline.
3. Slow Internet speeds at home are an excuse for shirking.
4. Programmes for older children air in the morning and evening.
5. All students are more productive in a physical classroom.

II Reading Comprehension

Read the text and then answer the following questions.

1. Why was Mr. Lin anxious about his son's online learning?
2. What can students do if connections are too wobbly for video calls?
3. How can students study in poor rural areas, where some households lack Internet access?
4. Who felt disruption most keenly?
5. How do you understand the statement "When schools and universities eventually re-open, classrooms may be different"?

III Discussion

Discuss the following questions based on the text.

1. How do you feel about online learning? In what ways can its efficiency be improved?
2. What's your ideal way of learning at present and in the future?

IV Writing

Write an essay according to the following directions.

Think about the advantages and disadvantages of online learning. Write an essay in no less than 250 words.

Ⓥ Translation

Translate the following passage from English to Chinese.

China will resume international cooperation in education following strict pandemic prevention and control measures, a senior education official said on Tuesday. Liu Jin, director of the Ministry of Education's department of international cooperation and exchange, said that with the COVID-19 pandemic raging globally, the ministry will conduct educational cooperation online. In the 14th Five-Year Plan period (2021–2025), the country will make new breakthroughs in advancing international educational cooperation in regions including Hainan Province, the Guangdong-Hong Kong-Macao Greater Bay Area, the Yangtze River Delta and Xiong'an New Area, Liu said at a news conference in Beijing. It will also continue to encourage students to study abroad to cultivate internationally competitive talent that can contribute to China's development, while improving the quality of education for international students studying in China, she said.

Ⓥ Project

Work in groups and report the merits and drawbacks of online and off-line learning at home and abroad. Then make a presentation in class.

Text B

Should All Countries Use the Shanghai Maths Method?

By Harry Low

When the Chinese city of Shanghai took part in the three-yearly PISA test of 15-year-olds' academic ability in 2009 and 2012, it topped the table in maths, leaving countries such as Germany, the UK, and the US—and even Singapore and Japan—trailing in its wake. What is its secret?

The life of a teacher in a Shanghai primary school differs quite a bit from that of teachers in most other countries. For one thing each teacher specialises in a particular subject—if you teach maths, you teach only maths.

These specialist teachers are given at least five years of training targeted at specific age groups, during which they gain a deep understanding both of their subject and of how children learn.

After qualifying, primary school teachers will typically take just two lessons per day, spending the rest of their time assisting students who require extra help and discussing teaching techniques with colleagues.

"If you compare that to an English practitioner in a primary school now, they might have five days of training in their initial teacher training year, if they're doing the School Direct route, for example," says Ben McMullen, head teacher of Ashburnham Community School, London. "They might have some follow-up training during the first or second year of training—inset, staff meetings etcetera—but there's no comparison between the expertise of someone who's had five years of training in a specific subject to someone who's had only a handful of days."

It's a similar story in secondary schools, where teachers spend less time in the classroom with pupils than they do on planning and refining lessons.

There are other differences too. School days are longer—from 07:00 until 16:00 or 17:00. Class sizes are larger. And lessons are shorter—each is 35 minutes long, followed by 15 minutes of unstructured play.

There is no streaming according to ability and every student must understand before the teacher moves on. In the early years of school, basic arithmetic is covered more slowly than in the UK, says McMullen, who has travelled to Shanghai in one of the groups of British teachers sent every year by the Department of Education to watch and learn.

"They looked at our curriculum and were horrified by how much we were trying to teach," he says.

"They wouldn't teach fractions until year four or five. By that time, they assume that the children were very fluent in multiplication and division."

"This is essentially a 'teaching for mastery' approach: covering less and making smaller incremental movements forward, ensuring the class move together as one and that you go over stuff again and again until it's truly understood."

It seems that other cities in China mainland may not be on quite the same level as Shanghai. In the 2015 PISA test Shanghai was bundled together with Beijing, Jiangsu and Guangdong, and they jointly came fifth in maths, behind Singapore, Japan, Taiwan (China) and Hong Kong (China).

It's also been suggested that Shanghai's results in previous years could have been skewed by the failure to include about a quarter of pupils in the city. However PISA insists its results demonstrate that the children of menial workers in Shanghai outperform the children of professionals in the West.

This is one of the key attractions of the system—it helps poor children realise their potential, increasing social mobility. But there are also drawbacks, according to Henrietta Moore of the Institute for Global Prosperity at University College London.

"The idea there is that effort brings rewards and so you will get this totally driven sort of idea but what you don't get—and what Chinese maths teachers are currently grappling with—is this creative problem-solving that requires space and mulling and dwelling," she says.

"We're actually much better at this in the UK and they're trying to develop that and learn from us."

Another criticism of the system is that parents work children too hard. An estimated 80% of students receive private lessons outside school.

"One of the downsides of parental interest in education is they get competitive—they're more competitive than the children—so they want to have all these extra classes," says Moore.

So is this a system other countries would do well to adopt?

"I would adopt the idea that anyone who teaches maths needs a deep understanding of the conceptual building of maths and a deep understanding of how children learn that," says Anne Watson, emeritus professor of maths teaching at Oxford University. "I would also want

to take on board the idea of high expectations for everyone."

Online entrepreneur Martha Lane-Fox is also a fan.

"Two things really appeal to me about this," she says. "The idea that everyone can be more of a maths master than I think we believe here in the UK. I also really like the incredible attention to the micro-detail. I'm really interested in this notion of incrementalism and moving things on in small chunks.

"The fundamentals of this policy are right and it's incredibly inspiring to think everybody can become more freed up by maths."

Ben McMullen's primary school has already been borrowing some of Shanghai's ideas, he says.

There is no streaming, pupils are interacting more and there is a "different atmosphere" in class.

"The younger learners moving up the school have an incredibly robust sense of maths, calculation and of concept," McMullen says.

And for teachers there is another great upside, he says—less marking.

 Words and Expressions

1. trail in its wake 尾随其后
2. **practitioner:** someone who regularly does a particular activity 从事者，实践者
3. **etcetera:** the full form of etc. 等等（etc. 的完整形式）
4. **expertise:** special skills or knowledge in a particular subject, that you learn by experience or training 专门技能
5. **streaming:** a method of transmitting data from the Internet directly to a user's computer screen without the need to download it 分流
6. **arithmetic:** the science of numbers involving adding, multiplying, etc. 算术
7. **curriculum:** the subjects that are taught by a school, college, etc. or the things that are studied in a particular subject 课程
8. **fraction:** a part of a whole number in mathematics, such as ½ or ¾（数学上的）分数
9. **incremental:** increasing in amount or value gradually and by a regular amount（定额）增长的
10. **bundle together** 捆绑
11. **skewed:** An opinion, piece of information, result, etc. that is skewed is incorrect, especially

because it has been affected by a particular thing or because you do not know all the facts. 偏颇的

12. **menial:** Menial work is boring, needs no skill, and is not important. （工作）枯燥的，无需技术的，不重要的

13. **social mobility** 社会流动

14. **grapple with** 尽力解决，设法理解（难题）

15. **mull:** to think about a problem, plan, etc. for a long time before making a decision 认真琢磨，反复思考

Cultural Notes

1. **PISA:** The Program for International Student Assessment is an international assessment that measures 15-year-old students' reading, mathematics, and science literacy every three years. First conducted in 2000, the major domain of study rotates between reading, mathematics, and science in each cycle. PISA also includes measures of general or cross-curricular competencies, such as collaborative problem solving. 国际学生评价项目

2. **Ashburnham Community School:** It is located in Chelsea area of London and is situated between the Thames and King's Road. The school offers fully funded places for students up to primary level and does not charge any fee for routine learning process, but parents have to pay some charges for after-school clubs and annual tours. The school actively involves children in different activities so that they can use their creativity and interests to learn more, and they can become an active part of the community where they live. Speech therapy services are also offered for students who do not speak English as their first language and specialized language teachers work hard to improve the language skills. 阿什伯纳姆社区学校

3. **Henrietta Moore:** Professor Henrietta L. Moore is the Founder and Director of the Institute for Global Prosperity and the Chair in Culture Philosophy and Design at University College London (UCL). A leading global thinker on prosperity, Professor Moore challenges traditional economic models of growth arguing that to flourish communities, businesses and governments need to engage with diversity and work within environmental limits. 亨利埃塔·摩尔

Exercises

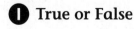 **True or False**

Read the text and make a judgment of the following statements.

1. When the Chinese city of Shanghai took part in the three-yearly PISA test of 15-year-olds' academic ability in 2009 and 2012, it topped the table in maths.

2. The specialist teachers are given at least five years of training targeted at different age groups.
3. In the early years of school, basic arithmetic is covered more quickly in China than in the UK.
4. It seems that other cities in Chinese mainland may not be on quite the same level as Shanghai.
5. There is streaming, pupils are interacting more and there is a "different atmosphere" in class.

II Reading Comprehension

Read the text and then answer the following questions.

1. What's the difference between the life of a teacher in a Shanghai primary school and that of teachers in most other countries?
2. How do you understand a "teaching for mastery" approach?
3. What is the one of the key attractions of the system?
4. What is the criticism of the system?
5. Why has McMullen's primary school already been borrowing some of Shanghai's ideas?

III Discussion

Discuss the following questions based on the text.

1. Should all countries use the Shanghai maths teaching method? What is your opinion?
2. What are the advantages and disadvantages of the Shanghai maths teaching method? Do you know any other effective teaching method at home and abroad?

IV Writing

Write an essay according to the following directions.

It is more important to study a subject that interests you than a subject preparing you for a better job or career. Do you agree or disagree? Write an essay in no less than 250 words.

V Translation

Translate the following passage from English to Chinese.

The Shanghai math pedagogy has in the past decade gained recognition around the world for helping the city to become top for math in the Organization for Economic Cooperation and Development's program for international student assessment rankings for students aged 15 and

16 years old in 2009 and 2012. During this period, the UK government was also looking at different ways to improve math knowledge in the country, and it eventually decided to adopt some elements of Shanghai math instruction in the local curriculum.

Ⅵ Project

Debate over the Chinese learning style and the US learning style.

Proposition: The Chinese learning style is better than the US learning style.

Opposition: The US learning style is better than the Chinese learning style.

Text C

China's English Language Ranking Improves

By Zhao Xinying

The English proficiency of people in China has reached its highest level since 2011, according to a report released on Wednesday in Shanghai.

The proficiency ranking rose three places to 36th among 80 countries and regions, according to the 2017 English Proficiency Index of the Swedish education company Education First, which has produced the report for seven years.

Proficiency in English among residents of Shanghai has ranked first in China for four consecutive years, followed by Hong Kong and Beijing, the report said.

The report is based on the EF Standard English Test results of more than 1 million people from 80 non-English-speaking countries and regions around the world.

Nine out of 10 people who took the test, which was developed by the company and consists of reading and listening, were not clients of Education First. The median age was 26; 48 percent of them were women.

The English proficiency of people in 80 percent of China's provinces and regions has improved since last year, thanks to education reforms adopted by the government, said Melissa Lam, general manager and chief representative of Education First in China.

"A lot of international conferences have been held in China in the past few years, which I think has helped with not only economic development but also with the development of English proficiency," she said.

Another notable finding is that the English proficiency of people in Fujian Province has risen steadily over the past few years and entered China's top five for the first time.

"Fujian's proficiency ranking has gone steadily upward," Lame said. "We can see that the province is on the 21st-Century Maritime Silk Road," Lam said. "It also hosted the 2017 BRICS Summit. So Fujian Province has experience and a reason to support increased English proficiency."

Cai Jigang, a professor of English at Shanghai's Fudan University, said the great investment made in English education by the Chinese government and society since 1978 has been the key. However, the test-oriented teaching approach remains, resulting in weak spoken English among many Chinese people, he said.

To change that, Lam suggested that English education in China should focus on communication rather than on mastering grammar. Constant exposure to English in daily life and technology-assisted learning are strongly recommended, she said.

Unit 6

Chinese Families

导读

中国电视剧《都挺好》的热播引发了热议。《都挺好》撕开了亲情的"遮羞布",探讨了重男轻女、啃老、不和谐的夫妻关系、愚孝的父子关系等这些中国家庭讳莫如深、难以启齿的议题。编剧王三毛说:"原生家庭欠你的,你得靠自己找回来。找不回来就是一场灾难,找回来就'都挺好'。"国内外对于家庭中的此类议题有什么不同的看法?对于"孝顺",中西方有怎样的看法?中国在2015年开始试行并在2016年全面开放"二孩政策"。随着这一政策的出台,不少中国家庭拥有了两个孩子,也有不少家庭依然选择只生养一个孩子。中国家庭对于全面开放的"二孩政策"有怎样的反应?哪些因素决定家庭生养孩子的数量?通过阅读本单元的文章,我们会有所思考和发现。

Text A

Conflicted Confucians

By an anonymous author

It is no mean feat to be one of the top-ten trending hashtags on Weibo, China's equivalent of Twitter, for 20 consecutive days and counting. *All Is Well*, a show on provincial television which premiered on March 1st, has done just that. The show tells the story of a fictional Chinese family torn by internal conflict. The female protagonist, Su Mingyu, is barely on speaking terms with her widowed father and one of her two brothers. The father is a nagging crank who expects his two adult sons to bankroll his lavish tastes. This leads to constant bickering between the brothers, neither of whom wants to be called "unfilial".

Episodes of *All Is Well* have been streamed more than 390m times. That exceeds the online viewership of the next most popular television series by 278m. From *The Simpsons* to *Game of Thrones*, dramas about bickering families are common in many countries. The questioning of blind attachment to traditional values in *All Is Well* is causing a stir. Viewers are transfixed by its rare portrayal of middle-class life, warts and all.

Many Chinese can relate to the Su family's troubles. The daughter holds a grudge against her father, and especially against her late mother, for having mistreated her while pampering her brothers. As a child she was made to wash her brothers' clothes. Her parents turned a blind eye when one of her brothers beat her. For many female viewers born before 1979, when China introduced a one-child-per-couple policy (changed to two in 2016), such scenes have brought back painful memories. Some have used social media to share their own tales of sexism within the family.

But the biggest reaction has been to the drama's critique of filial piety. Even today, the Confucian principle of unswerving loyalty to one's parents remains hallowed. Many people say the best measure of adherence to this virtue is whether a son takes good care of his parents in old age. A recent poll by Toutiao, a Chinese news app found that 54% of elderly people in China get more than half of their expenses covered by their adult children. Partly, no doubt, this is due to a patchy pensions system. But it also reflects a culture of "never saying no to your parents", says an *All Is Well* fan in Beijing.

In the series, however, the widowed father does not attract much sympathy. He throws tantrums and insists that his eldest son buy him a three-bedroom apartment (the son grudgingly does so). Commentators on social media have taken to calling the father *juying* ("giant baby")—a characteristic common among parents in real life, they say. The Su children do their duty, but the audience is supposed to applaud the resentment they express.

There have been mixed reviews in state media. One newspaper said that the "realistic plot and acting" had touched the "pain points" of many viewers. *Beijing Daily*, however, said the drama was "unrealistic". It said it caricatured elderly parents by "unreasonably" ascribing "every possible bad quality" of old people to one character.

Words and Expressions

1. **no mean feat** 绝非易事
2. **hashtag:** a word in a Twitter/Weibo message with # in front of it, which indicates what the message is about. People can search for hastags in order to find messages about a particular subject. 标签、话题
3. **consecutive:** Consecutive numbers or periods of time follow one after the other without any interruptions. 连续的
4. **premiere:** the first public performance of a film, play, or piece of music（电影的）首映；（戏剧、乐曲等的）首演
5. **bicker:** to argue, especially about something very unimportant（尤指为琐事）争吵，发生口角
6. **stir:** a feeling of excitement or annoyance 激动（情绪）；愤怒（情绪）
7. **grudge:** a feeling of dislike for someone because you cannot forget that they harmed you in the past 怀恨、怨恨
8. **pamper:** to look after someone very kindly, for example by giving them the things that they want and making them feel warm and comfortable 宠、娇惯
9. **filial:** relating to the relationship of a son or daughter to their parents 子女的；孝顺的
10. **tantrum:** a sudden short period when someone, especially a child, behaves very angrily and unreasonably 脾气发作
11. **caricature:** to draw or describe someone or something in a way that makes them seem silly 用漫画表现（讽刺）

Cultural Notes

1. *The Simpsons:* It is an animated Sitcom about the antics of a dysfunctional family called the Simpsons. Homer is the oafish unhealthy beer loving father, Marge is the hardworking homemaker wife, Bart is the ten-year-old underachiever (and proud of it), Lisa is the unappreciated eight-year-old genius, and Maggie is the cute, pacifier loving silent infant. 《辛普森一家》

2. *Game of Thrones:* It is an American fantasy drama television series created for HBO by David Benioff and D. B. Weiss. It is an adaptation of *A Song of Ice and Fire,* George R. R. Martin's series of fantasy novels, the first of which is titled *A Game of Thrones.* The episodes are mainly written by Benioff and Weiss, who are the executive producers alongside Martin, who writes one episode per season. Filmed in a Belfast studio and on location elsewhere in Northern Ireland, Malta, Scotland, Croatia, Iceland, the United States and Morocco, it premiered on HBO in the United States on April 17, 2011. Two days after the fourth season premiered in April 2014, HBO renewed *Game of Thrones* for a fifth and sixth season.《权力的游戏》

3. **one-child-per-couple policy:** In 1979, China reinforced its population control efforts by introducing the one-child-per-couple (OCPC) policy. This policy aimed at controlling China's population growth through drastic fertility reduction. 独生子女政策

Exercises

I True or False

Read the text and make a judgment of the following statements.

1. It is hard to be one of the top-ten trending hashtags on Weibo, China's equivalent of Twitter, for 20 consecutive days and counting.
2. Viewers are attracted by its rare portrayal of middle-class life, warts and all.
3. Many Chinese cannot understand the Su family's troubles.
4. Even today, the Confucian principle of unswerving loyalty to one's parents is still holly.
5. There have been different reviews of the show in state media.

II Reading Comprehension

Read the text and then answer the following questions.

1. What's the cause of constant bickering between the brothers?
2. What does the text tell us about the sexism in the Su family?
3. Why can many Chinese relate to the Su family's troubles?
4. What's the best measure of adherence to filial piety according to many people?
5. Why does the widowed father not attract much sympathy?

III Discussion

Discuss the following questions based on the text.

1. How do you view the virtue of filial piety in China?

2. How do you view the relationship between parents and children in the Western countries?

IV Writing

Write an essay according to the following directions.

Write a short essay on how to best handle the relationship between parents and children in no less than 250 words.

V Translation

Translate the following passage from English to Chinese.

But the biggest reaction has been to the drama's critique of filial piety. Even today, the Confucian principle of unswerving loyalty to one's parents remains hallowed. Many people say the best measure of adherence to this virtue is whether a son takes good care of his parents in old age. A recent poll by Toutiao, a Chinese news app found that 54% of elderly people in China get more than half of their expenses covered by their adult children. Partly, no doubt, this is due to a patchy pensions system. But it also reflects a culture of "never saying no to your parents", says an *All Is Well* fan in Beijing.

VI Project

Work in groups and trace the history of your family and share the stories of your family. You will have a "family sharing time" in the class.

Text B

One Child or Two? That Is the Question

By China Daily

BEIJING—Though often labeled one of China's most draconian laws, China's one-child policy, introduced at the end of the 1970s and abandoned at the beginning of 2016, achieved what it set out to do—rein in growth of the country's already vast population.

More than three decades on, as economic prosperity and nature have taken their course, the country faces a new demographic issue: it looks set to become old before it becomes rich.

Shi Hua, 37, was over the moon when his second daughter was born last month, but he is less than elated about how having a second child will affect his families' annual expenses. He estimates that this new addition to the family will cost around 20,000 yuan (2,900 U.S. dollars) every year.

"Money is not even our biggest concern. We are more worried about ensuring our kids are accepted into the best state schools," Shi said.

"Having two children means that neither will be lonely as they grow up, but even if the government allowed it, I wouldn't want more. Two is more than enough," Shi said.

Since January 1, 2016, all married couples have been allowed to have two children, following an earlier easing of the policy in 2013 allowing couples to have a second child if either parent was an only child.

Despite these measures, and allowances for ethnic groups and rural couples, China is facing a labor shortage. In 2015, China had just over 1 billion people of working age, but this is set to decline to 958 million in 2030 and 827 million in 2050, according to the Family Planning Association (FPA).

FPA vice president Wang Pei'an said that the government, concerned by the demographic shift, realized that the country could not afford to wait any longer to adjust its family planning policy.

"Do Not Dare"

A son and a daughter form the Chinese character "hao", which means good. Although Zheng Juan, 34, who works and lives in Tianjin Municipality, would like to have a second child to achieve a balanced "hao", she has neither the desire nor the support to extend her family.

"My parents have taken care of my daughter since she was born in 2011, as my husband and I both work," she said. "They are too old to take care of another child and we can't afford a good nanny."

Like Shi, education is also a concern for Zheng. To make sure her family are in the catchment area for a good primary school, Zheng bought a 2.5 million yuan apartment last year near her office so that she can manage the school runs.

According to a survey by the All-China Women's Federation (ACWF), of 10,000 families with children under 15 years old in 10 provincial-level regions, 53.3 percent expressed no desire to have a second child.

The key factors for most parents when considering a second child are the quality of schools, baby products, living environment and access to medical facilities. Other major considerations included whether a later pregnancy would be safe for the mother, if the family could even afford another child, and child care prior to kindergarten.

Chen Xiaoxia, head of the child division of the ACWF, said that financial considerations alone mean a considerable number of families "do not dare or want" to have a second child.

"Families that have a second child have new demands. They need advice and guidance," Chen said.

Support Now, Beyond

In the first half of 2016, 8.31 million babies were born in China, up 6.9 percent year on year. Of these newborns, 44.6 percent were a second child, up 6.7 percent, according to the FPA.

From December 2015, about 30,000 women registered to have children in Beijing, yet the city only has about 4,900 maternal beds and is capable of serving only 25,000 women.

According to Peking Union Medical College Press 2015 health statistics yearbook, China only has 0.43 pediatricians for every 1,000 children.

The relaxation of the family planning policy means that China will need 89,000 more maternity beds, and 140,000 more obstetricians and midwives by 2020, according to the National Health and Family Planning Commission.

Different provinces have set the wheels in motion to support women who want to have a second child, with plans in the pipeline to offer them longer paid maternal leave.

In developed countries, where women have the opportunity of education level and salaries on par with or near to their male counterparts, young people's lifestyles—and their interest in marrying or having children—have radically shifted, resulting in many women putting off having children until their mid-30s, if at all.

The two-child policy is "not the end" of family planning reform, according to the "Report on China's Population and Labor", issued by the Chinese Academy of Social Sciences in late November 2016.

In order to avoid a "low birth rate trap", China will continue to observe its demographic data and will take measures to intervene should it need to further relax its family planning policy. The recent reform of the family planning policy, if anything, marked the birth of a new era.

 ## Words and Expressions

1. **draconian:** very strict and cruel 严厉的，严酷的
2. **rein in:** to start to control a situation more strictly 严加控制
3. **demographic:** relating to the population and groups of people in it 人口的；人口统计的
4. **over the moon:** very happy 欣喜若狂的
5. **elated:** extremely happy and excited 兴高采烈的
6. **municipality:** a town, city or other small area, which has its own government to make decisions about local affairs, or the officials in that government 市；镇；区
7. **catchment area** 生源地，来源地
8. **pediatrician:** a doctor who deals with children and their illnesses 儿科医生
9. **maternity:** relating to a woman who is pregnant or who has just had a baby 产妇的
10. **obstetrician:** a doctor who has special training in obstetrics 产科医生
11. **midwife:** a specially trained nurse whose job is to help women when they are having a baby 助产士，接生员
12. **set the wheels in motion** 开展
13. **pipeline:** a line of connecting pipes, often under the ground, used for sending gas, oil etc. over long distances (用于长距离输送气体、石油等的地下) 管道、管线
14. **intervene:** to become involved in an argument, fight or other difficult situation in order to change what happens 干预、介入、插手

 ## Cultural Note

All-China Women's Federation (ACWF): formerly All-China Democratic Women's Foundation (1949–1957) and Women's Federation of the People's Republic of China (1957–1978), the official, state-sponsored organization representing women's interests in the People's Republic of China (PRC). Founded on April 3, 1949, the basic mission of the All-China

Unit 6 Chinese Families

Women's Federation's is to represent and safeguard the rights and interests of women and promote gender equality. The ACWF has advocated policy changes on behalf of women and also has played a role in responding to women's issues at a local level. Among its current tasks are to promote and increase literacy rates, technical skills, employment opportunities, family welfare, poverty alleviation, and the political participation of women.
中华全国妇女联合会（全国妇联）

Exercises

❶ True or False

Read the text and make a judgment of the following statements.

1. China's one-child policy controlled the growth of the country's already vast population.
2. Money is the family's biggest concern.
3. China only has 4.3 pediatricians for every 1,000 children.
4. The relaxation of the family planning policy means that China has already had enough resources for the second baby.
5. In developed countries, women's interest in marrying or having children has radically changed.

❷ Reading Comprehension

Read the text and then answer the following questions.

1. What is China's new demographic issue?
2. What are the key factors for most parents when considering a second child?
3. What support can women get if they want to have a second child?
4. Why do many women in developed countries put off having children until their mid-30s?
5. What will China do to avoid a "low birth rate trap"?

❸ Discussion

Discuss the following questions based on the text.

1. Why does the birth rate decrease nowadays in China? What can China do to raise its birth rate?
2. Some people enjoy a lifestyle of DINK (Double Income No Kids). Do you think it is necessary for a family to have a child?

Ⅳ Writing

Write an essay according to the following directions.

China has decided to end its decades-long one-child policy. All couples are allowed to have two children. This decision has aroused much chatter—whether it is high time that China should carry out the universal two-child policy or not. Write an essay in no less than 250 words.

Ⅴ Translation

Translate the following passage from English to Chinese.

The two-child policy is "not the end" of family planning reform, according to the "Report on China's Population and Labor", issued by the Chinese Academy of Social Sciences in late November 2016. In order to avoid a "low birth rate trap", China will continue to observe its demographic data and will take measures to intervene should it need to further relax its family planning policy. The recent reform of the family planning policy, if anything, marked the birth of a new era.

Ⅵ Project

Work in groups and trace the history of China's one-child policy and then make a presentation in class.

Text C

Chinese Parents Are Always Watching

By Li Yan

In China, it is common to see children attending extracurricular classes, playing instruments, or simply doing their homework with their parents by their side, looking over them.

Many Chinese parents spend all their energy and money on their children, sacrificing their own career and hobbies, all in the hope their children can have a good future.

Some parents accompany their children long after they've become adults. Media have widely reported that for nearly 10 years, Chinese parents have been planting vegetables in a deserted field near Yale University in their free time. When their children went abroad to study, their parents went with them, rented houses nearby the university and did housework for their children.

Feng Yan is one of these parents. On Saturdays, she has to get up at 6:30 a.m. to prepare breakfast for her son. Then she wakes him up, so he won't be late for his extracurricular classes at 8 a.m.

Her son is a sophomore in high school and is facing *gaokao* (college entrance exam) in a year.

When her son entered high school, Feng rented a house nearby to take better care of him and make it easier for him to focus on his studies. She said about 60 percent of students' parents rent apartments next to the high school.

Feng started planning her son's "academic career" a long time ago. When he was in elementary school, she took him to all sorts of math and English training classes on the weekends. In the evenings, she made her son practice violin and drawing.

She quit her job five years ago, when her son was in middle school, and started devoting her whole life to taking care of him.

"I feel very tired accompanying my son every day, but I've got no choice," Feng said.

Some children have expressed anxiety over their parents' full-time supervision. A third-grade student told the *Tianjin Daily*, "My mother is more familiar with my textbooks than me... if I did poorly on my exams, I think she'll be the most depressed person."

Education experts say constantly accompanying children can have negative effects. It's easy for the children to grow overly reliant on their parents. Besides, it's difficult for them to achieve their full potential when facing this amount of pressure.

Chinese Movies and Domestic Movie Market

导读

  在全球范围内叫好又卖座的大片，在中国的市场反馈却不如预期。是中国人的电影审美与众不同吗？事实上，中国电影变得越来越独特和自信，进口电影在中国的收益却在逐年下降。多年来，好莱坞制片人已经投入了大量资金。他们认为美国观众和中国观众并没有太大区别，都会为同一部精心打造的全球化电影欢笑、哭泣和欢呼。但中国观众总能证明他们错了。

Text A

Weak Tea Doesn't Sell
—A Chinese-American film star explains why blandly globalized fare flops in China

By The Economist

Even if it did not boast a character called Captain America, the superhero film *Avengers: Endgame* is a very obviously American spectacle. Beyond its swagger and expensive special effects, the Marvel comic book film series, of which this is the final instalment, celebrates flawed, individualistic superheroes. That the film just broke Chinese box-office records for its opening weekend could lead outsiders to assume that the American and Chinese film markets—the world's two largest—are converging. In fact, China's film world is becoming more distinctive and self-confident.

Hollywood producers have bet fair sums of money, over the years, on the idea that American and Chinese audiences are not so very different, and will laugh, weep and cheer at the same, carefully globalized movies. China has a habit of proving them wrong. The *Avengers* series has a large but distinctive set of fans in China, who often say they love the films precisely because they identify with its misfit heroes, struggling with a harsh, judgmental world.

Over 1.7bn cinema tickets were sold in China last year, a domestic record. Most sales were driven by locally made hits in which the stories ranged from Chinese military heroics overseas (*Operation Red Sea*) to a bittersweet drama about cancer (*Dying to Survive*). Though Hollywood had a respectable 2018 worldwide, revenues in China for imported films were down year on year.

Before *Avengers: Endgame,* the world's most successful film this year had been a Chinese science-fiction epic, *Wandering Earth*. But it owed this mainly to its popularity at home. By the end of its American cinema release less than 1% of its revenues came from the American box office. Western reviewers struggled to relate to a film that involved saving the planet, and in which the only speaking role for a non-Chinese was given to a Russian.

Celina Horan, a Chinese-American actor, speaks with authority about the two film markets. Educated in Hong Kong, China, and at the London School of Economics, UK, she is fluent in Cantonese, English and Mandarin. Known professionally as Celina Jade and in China as Lu Jingshan, she played the female lead in *Wolf Warrior 2*, released in 2017 and to date the highest-grossing Chinese film ever.

It is a revealing hit. A patriotic action adventure set in war-torn Africa, *Wolf Warrior 2* depicts a lone Chinese commando rescuing Chinese and African hostages from wicked American mercenaries.

Chaguan met Ms. Jade in Beijing after her return from a work trip to Los Angeles, as she prepared to visit Norway for a television travel show. "Two years ago Hollywood producers sought projects that would work in both America and China," she says. That might involve adding a Chinese actress to an American blockbuster in a "decorative role". Now her American meetings are "all about China". By this she means co-productions using American know-how, but squarely aimed at Chinese audiences.

The actress would not mourn if Hollywood were to drop projects crafted to appeal to all cultures, and offend in none. She compares the approval process for such films to dipping the same tea bag in ten cups, then drinking from the last. On the Chinese side, she sees studios growing less anxious about foreign success: "Why serve the global market when there's so much demand here?"

She is unsurprised when crossover hits struggle. Whereas Ms. Jade's American side related to *Crazy Rich Asians*, she says her Chinese side found it over the top, and even "fantastical". "Chinese audiences like to see romantic heroes showing their love in subtle ways," she says. "It might be how he serves her food."

State planners are playing a role. China opened 9,303 cinema screens last year, says IHS Markit, a consultancy. Government targets are for 80,000 screens nationwide by 2020, up from 60,000 today. Some will struggle amid an over supply of screens and a shortage of good titles. But expansion has boosted the clout of smaller cities where audiences relish films with local themes.

Words and Expressions

1. **flop:** to be a complete failure（电影票房）成绩不佳
2. **swagger:** showing sth. in an extremely proud and confident way（电影）炫酷特效的
3. **distinctive:** having a quality or characteristic that makes sth. different and easily noticed 独特的
4. **misfit:** a person who is not accepted by a particular group of people, especially because their behavior or their ideas are very different 与环境格格不入的人
5. **judgmental:** If you say that someone is judgmental, you are critical of them because they form opinions of people and situations very quickly, when it would be better for them to wait until they know more about the person or situation. 妄下结论的
6. **hit:** a piece of film, music or play to be very successful 票房大热的电影

7. **revenue:** money that a company, organization, or government receives from people 营业收入（会计）

8. **blockbuster:** something very successful, especially a very successful book or film/movie 大片

9. **clout:** power and influence 影响力

10. **relish:** to get great pleasure from sth. 喜爱

 ## Cultural Notes

1. *Avengers* series: The Avengers are a fictional team of superheroes appearing in American comic books published by Marvel Comics. The Avengers have appeared in a wide variety of media outside of comic books, including several different animated television series and direct-to-video films. The Avengers also play a central role in the Marvel Cinematic Universe (MCU) being the focus in multiple MCU feature films, beginning with the eponymous 2012 live-action film, *The Avengers*, and followed by the sequels *Age of Ultron* (2015), *Infinity War* (2018), and *Endgame* (2019), the latter two of which were based on the storyline of *The Infinity Gauntlet*.《复仇者联盟》系列

2. **Marvel:** Marvel Comics is the brand name and primary imprint of Marvel Worldwide Inc., formerly Marvel Publishing, Inc. and Marvel Comics Group, a publisher of American comic books and related media. In 2009, The Walt Disney Company acquired Marvel Entertainment, Marvel Worldwide's parent company. The Marvel brand, which had been used over the years, was solidified as the company's primary brand. 漫威

3. *Operation Red Sea:* It is a 2018 Chinese action war film directed by Dante Lam and starring Zhang Yi, Huang Jingyu, Hai Qing, Du Jiang and Prince Mak. The film is loosely based on the evacuation of the 225 foreign nationals and almost 600 Chinese citizens from Yemen's southern port of Aden during late March in 2015 Yemeni Civil War. It is currently the fourth-highest-grossing ever in China and highest grossing Chinese film in 2018.《红海行动》

4. *Dying to Survive:* It is a 2018 Chinese comedy-drama film directed by Wen Muye in his feature film debut. The film is based on the real-life story of Lu Yong, a Chinese leukemia patient who smuggled cheap but unproven cancer medicine from India for 1,000 Chinese cancer sufferers in 2004.《我不是药神》

5. *Wolf Warrior 2:* It is a 2017 Chinese action film co-written, co-produced, and directed by Wu Jing, who also starred in the lead role. The film co-stars Celina Jade, Frank Grillo, Hans Zhang, and Wu Gang. The film tells a story of a loose cannon Chinese soldier named Leng Feng who takes on special missions around the world. In this sequel, he finds himself in an African country protecting medical aid workers from local rebels and vicious arms dealers. It is the highest-grossing non-English film of all time.《战狼2》

6. *Wandering Earth:* It is a 2019 Chinese science fiction film directed by Frant Gwo, loosely based on the 2000 novella *The Wandering Earth* by Liu Cixin. Set in the far future, it follows

a group of astronauts and rescue workers guiding the Earth away from an expanding Sun, while attempting to prevent a collision with Jupiter. It is China's third highest-grossing film of all time and the third highest-grossing non-English film to date.《流浪地球》

Exercises

I True or False

Read the text and make a judgment of the following statements.

1. *Avengers: Endgame* proved that the American and Chinese film markets are converging.
2. Chinese film market is the largest in the world.
3. It is becoming hard for imported films to gain profit in China.
4. Films like *Wandering Earth* will be accepted by American audiences.
5. Films with local themes are more likely to be favored by Chinese local audiences.

II Reading Comprehension

Read the text and then answer the following questions.

1. How do you understand the "weak tea" in the title of the text?
2. Why does blandly globalized fare flop in China?
3. What kind of movie has dominated the Chinese film market?
4. Why is it so hard for Western reviewers to appreciate *Wandering Earth*?
5. Summarize Lu Jingshan's view on the two film markets.

III Discussion

Discuss the following questions based on the text.

1. Does it work well to add a decorative role in an American blockbuster to please Chinese audiences?
2. Why do Chinese audience prefer movies with local themes?

IV Writing

Write an essay according to the following directions.

Describe the different tastes of films for different age groups in China. Write an essay in no less than 250 words.

Ⅴ Translation

Translate the following passage from English to Chinese.

Hollywood producers have bet fair sums of money, over the years, on the idea that American and Chinese audiences are not so very different, and will laugh, weep and cheer at the same, carefully globalized movies. China has a habit of proving them wrong. The *Avengers* series has a large but distinctive set of fans in China, who often say they love the films precisely because they identify with its misfit heroes, struggling with a harsh, judgmental world.

Ⅵ Project

Work in groups and search for data related to the box office in China and the US over the past five years. Then present your findings in class.

Text B

Why *Star Wars* Keeps Bombing in China
By Alan Yuhas

The assault was swift and sustained: 500 Stormtroopers stood on the Great Wall. X-Wings swooped into Shanghai and Beijing. Lightsabers crackled in theaters across the country.

And millions of moviegoers responded: This again? Who cares?

One after another, *Star Wars* movies have flopped in China, defying efforts to bring one of the most successful franchises in history into a market that has printed money for the heroes, monsters and robots of other films. The latest *Star Wars* movie, *The Rise of Skywalker*, has followed the trend by grossing nearly a billion dollars worldwide and barely breaking $20 million in China.

The episodes that came before it didn't do much better, for reasons that include history, geopolitics and a distinct lack of the nostalgia that drove viewers in the United States. Thousands of Americans lined up in costumes for each premiere: *The Force Awakens* opened to almost a quarter-billion dollars in the United States in 2015; two years later, *The Last Jedi* made nearly as much; and *The Rise of Skywalker* raked in $177 million in its first few days last month.

In China, those movies opened to $52 million, $28 million and $12 million, respectively.

Chen Tao, who manages China's biggest fan website, Star Wars Fans China, estimated that China's fan clubs have fewer than 200 members in all.

As ticket sales for *The Last Jedi* dwindled in China a few years ago, a college student in Beijing, Xu Meng, told *The South China Morning Post* that the filmmakers should try new stories, new characters—and a new name. "If the new *Star Wars* sequels were not named after *Star Wars*, it would be better," she said.

Another student, Lang Yifei, called the series "heavy and gloomy", adding: "I think they need to give up on the old stories."

The diminishing returns from the series in China are in spite of Disney's aggressive marketing efforts. The company deployed miniature Stormtroopers and life-size starfighters, and collaborated with Chinese partners on a host of projects, including translated books and a music video by a Chinese-Korean boy band.

The campaign underscores how much money is at stake in the Chinese film market, now the second largest in the world. The latest *Avengers* movie grossed more than half a billion dollars there, and series like *Transformers* and *The Fast and the Furious* consistently make hundreds of millions of dollars.

The difference, film historians and industry experts said, is that movies like *Hobbs & Shaw* or *Jurassic World* can mostly stand apart from the stories they followed, and that Chinese audiences have grown up with series like Marvel's comic-book heroes.

But almost no one in China grew up with the original *Star Wars*.

"That basically wiped out the first six films of the franchise," said Michael Berry, a professor of Chinese literature and film at the University of California, Los Angeles. "It didn't have the opportunity to get its hooks in."

With "somewhat abstruse, complicated jargons and plots", said Ying Xiao, a professor of China studies and film at the University of Florida, "it is quite difficult for a Chinese audience who was not raised along with sequels to comprehend, digest and appreciate the attraction."

And while the first three films inspired untold tons of merchandise—keeping interest alive after the credits rolled—the movies remained essentially unknown in China, except as picture storybooks that riffed on *Star Wars* images with no relation to the movies.

Parents did not pass action figures, lunchboxes or VHS tapes on to their children. By the time the prequel trilogy was released around the turn of the century, with Chinese theaters opening up, Skywalker was still a foreign word.

China's box office has recently been dominated by homegrown competitors, Ms. Xiao noted. Those include *Ip Man 4*, the latest in a martial arts saga, and *The Wandering Earth*, an example of "hard" science fiction that is more popular in China than the "science fiction soap opera" of *Star Wars*.

And over the last decade, China's film industry has matured across production, directing, marketing and acting, said Marc Ganis, the president of the entertainment company Jiaflix. He noted that *Star Wars* had struggled in other Asian countries with tougher competition at home, like Japan and South Korea.

For the *Star Wars* spinoff *Rogue One*, Disney filmmakers cast two stars well-known to Asian audiences—Donnie Yen and Jiang Wen—to small effect.

In a 2018 interview, Mr. Yen attributed the film's struggles in China to its long back story, which he compared with the relative simplicity—and success—of comic-book movies. "Marvel is a lot easier to understand," he said. "*Star Wars*, there's a whole universe out there."

As if to prove his point, *Avengers: Endgame* made more in its 2019 opening weekend in China than all the *Star Wars* premieres combined.

And some selling points of the original trilogy—like the special effects that awed audiences in the '70s and '80s—are more charming than revolutionary in the 21st century, said Aynne Kokas, a professor at the University of Virginia and the author of *Hollywood Made in China*.

"*Star Wars* in the West is really a kind of generational phenomenon," she said, "the experience of sharing your experience with your kids." She noted that the arc of the series was largely about family and full of callbacks, an evolving mythology and generational transitions.

"What we've seen is a lot of derivative activity, a lot of derivative characters, efforts to recapture the magic of the original trilogy," she said. "That hasn't caught on with audiences in China."

Ms. Kokas said that the character known as Baby Yoda, from the series *The Mandalorian*, was an example of the franchise trying to recreate its greatest hits. "Yoda is gone, and we're trying to bring the magic of *Star Wars* into the next generation," she said.

Words and Expressions

1. **assault:** the act of attacking a building, an area 攻击，突袭
2. **defy:** to refuse to obey 违抗
3. **premiere:** the first public performance of a film/movie or play 首映
4. **at stake** 十分重要
5. **trilogy:** a group of three books, films/movies, etc. that have the same subject or characters 三部曲
6. **prequel:** a book or a film/movie about events that happened before those in a popular book or film/movie 前传
7. **box office** 电影票房
8. **spinoff:** a book, film, or television series that comes after and is related to a successful book, film, or television series 续集，衍生作品
9. **recapture:** to win back a place, position 夺回

Cultural Notes

1. **Star Wars:** It is an American epic space opera media franchise created by George Lucas, which began with the eponymous 1977 film and quickly became a worldwide pop-culture phenomenon. It holds a Guinness World Records title for the "most successful film merchandising franchise". In 2020, its total value was estimated at US$70 billion, and it is currently the fifth-highest-grossing media franchise of all time.《星球大战》

2. **Stormtroopers:** The Stormtroopers are the elite shock troops/space marines of the Galactic Empire, under the leadership of Emperor Palpatine and his commanders, most notably Darth Vader and Grand Moff Tarkin, during the original film trilogy. 帝国冲锋队

3. **lightsaber:** A lightsaber is a fictional energy sword featured in the *Star Wars* franchise. A typical lightsaber is depicted as a luminescent blade of magnetically contained plasma about 3 feet (0.91 m) in length emitted from a metal hilt around 10.5 inches (27 cm) in length. 光剑

4. **Transformers:** It is a live-action film series started in 2007. It follows the battles of sentient, living autonomous robots, often the Autobots and the Decepticons, who can transform into other forms, such as vehicles and animals.《变形金刚》

5. **The Fast and the Furious:** The series consist of action films that are largely concerned with illegal street racing, heists and spies, and are distributed by Universal Pictures.《速度与激情》

Exercises

I True or False

Read the text and make a judgment of the following statements.

1. *Star Wars* movie flopped in Chinese film market.
2. Ticket sales for *Star Wars* series dwindled year after year.
3. It is quite difficult for any Chinese audience to appreciate the *Star Wars*.
4. *Star Wars* series comprises three movies.
5. *Star Wars* is regarded as a kind of generational phenomenon for the Western audiences.

II Reading Comprehension

Read the text and then answer the following questions.

1. Why *Star Wars* is so charming for Western audiences?
2. Why do Chinese young audience prefer *Avengers* to *Star Wars*.
3. Summarize Michael Berry's view.

4. Summarize Ying Xiao's view.
5. According to Aynne Kokas, why did *Star Wars* fail to catch on with audiences in China?

III Discussion

Discuss the following questions based on the text.

1. Homegrown competitors have dominated the Chinese box office. Does that mean Chinese movies have improved a lot in quality?
2. In China, is there a generational phenomenon like *Star Wars* in the US?

IV Writing

Write an essay according to the following directions.

Just like the hard landing of *Star Wars* in China, most of the Chinese films also flopped in other countries. Why is it so hard for foreign movies to enter another market? Write an essay in no less than 250 words.

V Translation

Translate the following passage from English to Chinese.

The diminishing returns from the series in China are in spite of Disney's aggressive marketing efforts. The company deployed miniature Stormtroopers and life-size starfighters, and collaborated with Chinese partners on a host of projects, including translated books and a music video by a Chinese-Korean boy band.

The campaign underscores how much money is at stake in the Chinese film market, now the second largest in the world. The latest *Avengers* movie grossed more than half a billion dollars there, and series like *Transformers* and *The Fast and the Furious* consistently make hundreds of millions of dollars.

VI Project

Are you a crazy fan of *Star Wars*? Share your own story with your classmates. Work in groups and try to figure out the influence of *Star Wars* among your peers.

Text C

China Challenges Hollywood with Own Sci-fi Blockbuster

By Lily Kuo

China has entered the cinematic space race. *Wandering Earth*, the country's first blockbuster sci-fi film, is on track to be one of the highest grossing films in China's history.

The film has brought in more than 2bn yuan (£232m) in the six days since its release on 5 February, lunar new year. So far, it is the highest grossing film released over the holiday season, a peak time for the Chinese box office.

Set in the distant future, the governments of Earth, confronted with annihilation from an unstable sun, have strapped thrusters on to the planet, ejecting it out into the universe in search of a new home. But as the Earth approaches Jupiter, a malfunction in the system puts it on course to crash into the planet.

Described as a cross between *Armageddon* and *2001: Space Odyssey*, the film is seen by some as the dawn of Chinese sci-fi—a genre that has long been dominated by Hollywood. Several other Chinese–made films set in space are set to debut this year, including *Shanghai Fortress*, an alien invasion of earth, and *Pathfinder*, which follows a spaceship that crashes into a deserted planet.

"2019 could be remembered as year zero of Chinese science fiction blockbusters. It is not just about one successful movie, but about the emergence of multiple films," Frant Gwo, the director of *Wandering Earth*, told the government web portal China.org.cn.

China is already home to a thriving science and speculative fiction literary scene. *Wandering Earth* is based on the work of Liu Cixin, the author of the *Three Body Problem* series and the first Chinese author to win the Hugo award.

"*Wandering Earth* fills the gap in Chinese science-fiction movies. It means that China's science fiction movies have officially set sail," one fan of the film wrote on the review site Douban.

Slow to get off the ground in the first few days of its release, the film received positive reviews for its special effects. For Chinese moviegoers, accustomed to sci-fi films made by US studios, Chinese elements like references to spring festival, or Chinese new year, mahjong, and road signs common in China ("Safety Comes First") were a welcome change.

Some noted that unlike many Chinese blockbusters, *Wandering Earth* dials back on the patriotism. Rescue teams from around the world scramble to get the thrusters back up and running. A Russian soldier sacrifices his life to help a Chinese colleague.

"This is not a patriotic film but a film about humans saving themselves," one reviewer said.

Unit 8

Chinese Online Celebrities

导读

　　自媒体时代造就了一大批"网红"。他们或因艺术才华一鸣惊人，或因搞怪作秀博人眼球，或者是通过网络推手精心策划、包装打造而成。网民和资本的狂欢造就了一批又一批的"网络红人"。在这片繁花似锦中，有人因中伤和争吵而倍感失望，也有人因为有数不清的自由选择而如鱼得水。

Text A

China's Viral Idol: A Girl Next Door with Fast-Talking Attitude

By Amy Qin

BEIJING—Jiang Yilei is the girl next door who rants about dieting and nagging parents in the living room of her cluttered apartment here. She has bangs, wears minimal makeup and keeps two cats.

She is also one of China's most sudden and popular online celebrities, better known as Papi Jiang. In less than a year, her business partners say, she has accumulated 44 million followers, across multiple platforms, with her fast-talking satirical videos.

Even though there is probably some overlap among platforms, that figure outstrips the followings of such popular YouTube celebrities as Ryan Higa (17.8 million) and Jenna Marbles (16.4 million).

Last month, Ms. Jiang's first live broadcast—a rambling, unscripted 90-minute video—was watched more than 74 million times in one day. That was more views than Taylor Swift's latest music video, "New Romantics", received on YouTube in four months.

True, most things in China are on a bigger scale than they are elsewhere. But even by Chinese standards, Ms. Jiang, 29, stands out, so much so that Chinese media outlets have taken to calling her the No. 1 online celebrity of 2016.

"Papi Jiang is by far the most popular online celebrity," said Kunkun Yu, chief executive of the Beijing-based online community app Linglong. "Many young Chinese people see her as their idol."

Ms. Jiang's meteoric rise reflects the fast-changing nature of the Chinese Internet and, in particular, its insatiable demand for content.

China's web has become increasingly mobile driven, with more than 92 percent of the country's 710 million Internet users now coming to the web via their mobile phones, according to a report published this month by the official China Internet Network Information Center. They are using the Internet to shop, chat with their friends and seek information and entertainment on apps like Weibo, a microblog platform, and WeChat, the social messaging app.

This has led to the growth of what Chinese have taken to calling "self-media", an umbrella term for self-posted content on social media platforms.

Yang Ming, Ms. Jiang's business partner and a former classmate at the Central Academy of Drama in Beijing, said in an interview, "We saw that self-media was getting pretty big, so we thought, 'Should we try to do something with this?'" (Ms. Jiang, who rarely speaks to the news media, declined to be interviewed.)

As recently as mid-2015, Mr. Yang said, not many people were making short videos in China, whereas in the United States, YouTube celebrities have been common for years. "They weren't even being called short videos at the time," he said. "They were just videos."

Ms. Jiang, who had returned to graduate school at the Central Academy of Drama after working in entertainment for several years, including as a stage actor and assistant director, started to experiment, playing with elements that would become part of her signature style: a digitally altered voice, rapid-fire delivery and jump cuts.

Slowly, she began building a following, until one day last November when a video she made, poking fun at Shanghai women and their tendency to drop English words into conversation, went viral.

"I was shocked, scared to death," she said in a June interview with the Chinese website Sina. "I thought, 'What am I going to do?' I couldn't even eat anything."

Since then, she has made about 60 videos that focus on subjects familiar to educated young urbanites, like cheating boyfriends, celebrity culture and regional dialects. In one memorable example, she sounds off on how she hates it when people in love constantly talk about their partners. In another, she takes on the issue of gender stereotyping in China.

"Things you have definitely heard at some point," she announces to the camera. "This job is too tiring. It's not suited for women." Jump cut. "Playing basketball? Women are better off at home." Jump cut. "A woman should have long hair." Jump cut. "Women dabbling in homosexuality is fine, but I can't stand it with men." Jump cut. "A male nurse? Ew."

She signs off in the two-minute video with what has become her catchphrase: "I'm Papi Jiang, a woman possessing both beauty and talent."

For her audience, made up mostly of 20- to 30-somethings in coastal cities, the Shanghai-born Ms. Jiang offers a fresh, urban perspective rarely seen in Chinese comedy.

"Before, you had popular stand-up comedians like Zhao Benshan, but it was often a very rural type of humor, with jokes about things like plowing fields and eating leeks," said Ms. Yu, the online community app executive.

She added: "Papi's appeal, on the other hand, is with the white-collar workers who want to talk about how they're 39 years old and not married yet, and what should they do."

As Ms. Jiang's popularity skyrocketed, Internet companies and investors began to notice.

In recent years, since the government began cracking down on pirated content, companies have been thirsty for high-quality original material made locally.

Against that background, Ms. Jiang's appeal as someone who writes, shoots and edits her own videos is clear.

In March, she became one of the first viral Chinese stars to attract venture capital, when a group made up of four major institutional investors announced that it was putting $1.8 million into her company.

"In its current form, the market has only seen a succession of short-lived online celebrities," one of those investors, Luo Zhenyu, the founder and host of a popular online talk show, told the Chinese online publication *The Paper*. "We're looking at a person who has unlimited potential to transform this market and bring a whole new business logic."

Having secured the investment, Ms. Jiang and her business partners are now focused on building up PapiTube, a content platform through which they have begun to support and develop other young content creators in China.

They may face difficulties, though. In April, China's top broadcast regulator ordered Ms. Jiang to clean up the occasional foul language in her videos, forcing her to take down most of them temporarily. That was widely seen as a message from the government that it wants to assert control over online celebrities.

But it apparently did not diminish her appeal. Just days after she was scolded by the censors, she auctioned an ad spot in one of her videos for $3.3 million to a Shanghai online makeup retailer. (She has said that she plans to donate the money to the Central Academy of Drama.)

With so much at stake, the big question is whether she can continue to produce quality material. Although she releases new videos every week, it seems that she is still getting accustomed to her celebrity status.

Asked in the Sina interview in June why she did not make an appearance on the day of the auction, she responded with just one word: "Nervous."

 Words and Expressions

1. **rant**: to speak or complain about sth. in a loud and angry way 怒吼，咆哮
2. **nagging**: complaining 唠唠叨叨的
3. **cluttered**: covered with, or full of, a lot of things or people, in a way that is untidy 凌乱的
4. **satirical**: using satire to criticize sb./sth. 讽刺的，讥讽的

Unit 8 Chinese Online Celebrities

5. **meteoric:** achieving success very quickly 迅速成功的
6. **insatiable:** always wanting more of sth.; not able to be satisfied 不知足的
7. **urbanite:** a resident of an urban community; city dweller 城市居民
8. **stereotyping:** a fixed idea or image that many people have of a particular type of person or thing, but which is often not true in reality 刻板印象
9. **catchphrase:** a popular phrase that is connected with the politician or entertainer who used it and made it famous 标志性话语，流行语
10. **skyrocket:** to rise quickly to a very high level 飞涨，猛涨
11. **viral:** to become popular quickly like the spreading of the virus 走红（指某种事物在互联网、媒体或者公众中快速传开）
12. **auction:** a public event at which things are sold to the person who offers the most money for them 拍卖

Cultural Notes

1. **Papi Jiang:** Jiang Yilei (born on February 17, 1987), known as the online moniker Papi Jiang, is a Chinese comedian known for her comedy on video blogs, where she pokes fun at everyday topics including entertainment news, dating and family relationships. Papi 酱（本名姜逸磊）

2. **Ryan Higa:** Ryan Higa (born on June 6, 1990), also known as nigahiga, is an American comedian, Internet personality, musician, and actor. He is known for his comedy videos on YouTube. His YouTube channel, nigahiga, was the most subscribed channel on YouTube for 677 consecutive days from 2009 to 2011. Higa was nominated for "Best Video Blogger" at the 6th Shorty Awards. 瑞安·比嘉

3. **Jenna Marbles:** Jenna Nicole Mourey (born on September 15, 1986), better known by her pseudonym Jenna Marbles, is an American YouTube personality, vlogger, comedian, and actress. Mourey is the first social media star to have a wax figure displayed at Madame Tussauds Museum in New York City. 詹娜·马布尔

4. **venture capital:** It is a form of private equity financing that is provided by venture capital firms or funds to startups, early-stage, and emerging companies that have been deemed to have high growth potential or which have demonstrated high growth. 风险投资

Exercises

I True or False

Read the text and make a judgment of the following statements.

1. Jiang Yilei ranks among the top YouTubers because of her charming appearance and personality.
2. Netizens in China are becoming keen on contented-based videos.
3. Jiang Yilei is appealing among educated young urbanites in China.
4. For a period of time, Jiang's videos are flooded with foul language.
5. Jiang Yilei is nervous about the future of her career.

II Reading Comprehension

Read the text and then answer the following questions.

1. What is Papi Jiang's core competence?
2. Why is Papi Jiang so popular among the young urbanites in China?
3. Why is it crucial for Papi Jiang to attract venture capital?
4. What is the whole new business logic mentioned by Luo Zhenyu? How do you understand it?
5. Do the audiences like the foul language in her videos or not?

III Discussion

Discuss the following questions based on the text.

1. Jiang Yilei's videos gained a considerable amount of likes across all platforms. Does it mean she has ranked among the top YouTubers?
2. What impression does Papi Jiang make on you?

IV Writing

Write an essay according to the following directions.

Write an essay on the influence of self-media (or we-media) among the millennials in China in no less than 250 words. You are expected to deliver a clear structure and strong supporting evidence.

Ⅴ Translation

Translate the following passage from English to Chinese.

China's web has become increasingly mobile driven, with more than 92 percent of the country's 710 million Internet users now coming to the web via their mobile phones, according to a report published this month by the official China Internet Network Information Center. They are using the Internet to shop, chat with their friends and seek information and entertainment on apps like Weibo, a microblog platform, and WeChat, the social messaging app.

Ⅵ Project

Debate over online celebrity economy.

Proposition: Online celebrity economy represents the future trend.

Opposition: Online celebrity economy is just a flash in the pan.

Text B

The Reclusive Food Celebrity Li Ziqi Is My Quarantine Queen

By Tejal Rao

Like so many home cooks in quarantine, after I've used up the green tops of my scallions, I drop the white, hairy roots into a glass of water to regenerate, feeling pleased with my own sense of thrift and pragmatism.

But last week, after the Chinese Internet star Li Ziqi posted a new cooking video to YouTube called "The Life of Garlic", I wished I could graduate from scallions on the windowsill.

In the 12-minute video, which already has over seven million views, Ms. Li pushes garlic cloves into a patch of earth outside her home. A time lapse shows the sprouts growing, reaching up toward the sky.

Ms. Li sautées the young, fresh green garlic shoots with pork. When she harvests the bulbs, she plaits the stems, hanging them up to finish the drying process, pickling and preserving the rest, and using some to season chicken feet and dress salad.

Ms. Li, who lives in a village in Sichuan Province and rarely speaks to press, looks not unlike a Disney princess in her crown braids, wearing a silvery fur cape, trudging gracefully in the snow. At 29, she is famous for her mesmerizing videos of rural self-sufficiency, posted on Weibo and YouTube.

For a worldwide audience in isolation, her D.I.Y. pastoral fantasies have become a reliable source of escape and comfort.

I usually plan to watch one—just one—but then I let the algorithm guide me to another, and another, until, soothed by bird song and instrumentals, I'm convinced that I'm absorbing useful information from Ms. Li about how to live off the land.

If I'm ever stuck with two dozen sweet potatoes, I now have some idea how to extract the starch and use it to make noodles. This is what I tell myself. Leave me alone in a lotus pond, and I know how to harvest and prepare the roots.

Ms. Li doesn't explain anything as she goes. In fact, she tends to work in silence, without the use of any modern kitchen gadgets. Her sieve is a gourd. Her grater is a piece of metal that she punctures, at an angle, then attaches to two pieces of wood. Her basin is a stream, where she washes the dirt from vegetables.

Her kitchen is nothing like mine, in Los Angeles. But watching Ms. Li on my laptop, while eating a bowl of buttered popcorn for dinner, I think maybe I could be happy living like that, too, soaking in the sheer natural beauty of the countryside, devoting myself to extremely traditional ways of cooking.

Ms. Li makes peach blossom wine and cherry wine, preserves loquats and rose petals. She makes fresh tofu, and Lanzhou-style noodle soup with a perfectly clear broth, and ferments Sichuan broad bean paste from scratch. She butchers ducks and whole animals.

She is not known for taking shortcuts. A video about matsutake mushrooms begins with her building the grill to cook them, laying the bricks down one at a time, scraping the mortar smooth, then hunting for mushrooms in the woods.

In a video about cooking fish, she first goes fishing, in the snow, patiently throwing back any catches that are too small, as snowflakes freeze into her hair.

Like the main character in some kind of post-apocalyptic novel, Ms. Li is almost always alone, though she doesn't seem lonely, riding her horse through fields of wildflowers, or carrying baskets of sweet potatoes under citrus trees. She seems tireless, focused, confident, independent.

The videos are deeply soothing. But it's not just that—they reveal the intricacy and intensity of labor that goes into every single component of every single dish, while also making the long, solitary processes of producing food seem meaningful and worthwhile.

It's the complete opposite of most cooking content, the kind that suggests that everything is so quick and easy that you can do it, too, and probably in less than 30 minutes.

But Ms. Li also romanticizes the struggles of farm life, and, as any savvy influencer would, monetizes that appeal. In her online shop, she sells a curved cleaver, similar to the ones she uses in her videos, as well as loose Hanfu-inspired linen clothing, Sichuan ginseng honey and chile sauces.

Ms. Li's story, as she tells it, is that she left home as a teenager to find work, but returned to the countryside to take care of her grandmother, then began documenting her life. Though she used to shoot her videos alone, on her phone, she now works with an assistant and a videographer.

"I simply want people in the city to know where their food comes from," Ms. Li said, in a rare interview with Goldthread last fall. (She never responded to my requests.)

But most of the world's food, whether in China or the United States, doesn't come from anyone's backyard, and isn't made from scratch. Noodles are produced and packaged in factories. Chickens and pigs are gutted on fast, dangerous lines.

The fragility of our industrial supply chains, and the immense risks for the people who work in commercial plants and slaughterhouses, have been laid bare in the last few weeks.

Ms. Li sidesteps the existence of that broken system entirely. This is the powerful fantasy of her videos right now—people growing and cooking all of their own food, not wasting anything, and not needing anything more than what they already have around them.

In isolation, watching Ms. Li gather rose petals and ripe tomatoes, I catch myself thinking, is this sequence set in the past, or the future? Are these videos a record of the collective food knowledge we've already lost, or an idealized vision of its recovery?

 Words and Expressions

1. **reclusive:** living alone and deliberately avoiding the company of others 隐居的
2. **quarantine:** a period of time when an animal or a person that has or may have a disease is kept away from others in order to prevent the disease from spreading 隔离期
3. **thrift:** the habit of saving money and spending it carefully so that none is wasted 节约，节俭
4. **pragmatism:** thinking about solving problems in a practical and sensible way rather than by having fixed ideas and theories 实用主义，务实思想，实用观点
5. **windowsill:** a narrow shelf below a window, either inside or outside 窗沿，窗台
6. **lapse:** a period of time between two things that happen（两件事情发生的）间隔时间
7. **sauté:** to fry food quickly in a little hot fat 嫩煎
8. **mesmerizing:** attracting and holding interest as if by a spell 有吸引力的
9. **pastoral:** showing country life or the countryside, especially in a romantic way 田园的
10. **algorithm:** a set of rules that must be followed when solving a particular problem 计算机算法
11. **starch:** a white carbohydrate food substance found in potatoes, flour, rice 淀粉
12. **broth:** thick soup made by boiling meat or fish and vegetables in water 肉汤
13. **from scratch** 白手起家，从头开始
14. **intricacy:** the fact of having complicated parts, details or patterns 错综复杂
15. **savvy:** practical knowledge or understanding of sth. 实际知识；见识

Cultural Notes

1. **YouTube:** It is an American online video-sharing platform and now operates as one of Google's subsidiaries. YouTube allows users to upload, view, rate, share, add to playlists, report, comment on videos, and subscribe to other users. It offers a wide variety of user-generated and corporate media videos. Available content includes video clips, TV show clips, music videos, short and documentary films, audio recordings, movie trailers, live streams, and other contents such as video blogging, short original videos, and educational videos. 油管

2. **Li Ziqi:** a Chinese food and country-life blogger and online celebrity. She is known for creating food and handicraft preparation videos in her hometown of rural Pingwu, Mianyang, Sichuan, often from basic ingredients and tools using traditional Chinese techniques. 李子柒

3. **Weibo:** Sina Weibo is a Chinese microblogging website. Launched by Sina Corporation on 14 August 2009, it is one of the biggest social media platforms in China. In June 2020, Sina Weibo's active monthly users reached 523 million. 微博

Exercises

I True or False

Read the text and make a judgment of the following statements.

1. Ms. Li appears to be good at cooking.
2. The author really appreciates the country lifestyle.
3. After Ms. Li monetizes her appeal, followers tend to be dissatisfied.
4. Ms. Li's videos have drawn a vivid portrait of country lifestyle in China.
5. According to the author, the modern industrial supply chains are fragile.

II Reading Comprehension

Read the text and then answer the following questions.

1. What kind of lifestyle is shown in Ms. Li's videos?
2. Why are people living in metropolitan areas so fascinated with Ms. Li's videos?
3. Are overseas audiences attracted by Ms. Li's individual charisma or the country lifestyle?
4. How do you understand the fragility of our industrial supply chains?
5. What are your answers to the two questions posed in the last paragraph of the article: Is this sequence set in the past, or the future? Are these videos a record of the collective food knowledge we've already lost, or an idealized vision of its recovery?

Ⅲ Discussion

Discuss the following questions based on the text.

1. Do you think Ms. Li's videos reflect the reality of Chinese country life?
2. Is it appropriate for Internet influencers to monetize their appeal? Give your comments.

Ⅳ Writing

Write an essay according to the following directions.

The calmness of the countryside came as a welcome relief from the hustle and bustle of city life. Write an essay on the pastoral life in modern society in no less than 250 words.

Ⅴ Translation

Translate the following passage from English to Chinese.

Like the main character in some kind of post-apocalyptic novel, Ms. Li is almost always alone, though she doesn't seem lonely, riding her horse through fields of wildflowers, or carrying baskets of sweet potatoes under citrus trees. She seems tireless, focused, confident, independent.

The videos are deeply soothing. But it's not just that—they reveal the intricacy and intensity of labor that goes into every single component of every single dish, while also making the long, solitary processes of producing food seem meaningful and worthwhile.

Ⅵ Project

Work in groups to trace the life stories of Chinese Internet influencers. Then present your findings in class.

Text C

Brands Turn to China's Digital Influencers to Fuel Sales

By Louise Lucas

Gogoboi spent a month wearing outfits matching Pokémon characters. Yao Chen—China's answer to Angelina Jolie—hangs out with refugees. Papi Jiang swears way too much.

Meet China's key opinion leaders (KOLs). Like America's YouTube stars, they are a diverse bunch who range from the girl next door to renowned actors. They boast millions of followers—80m in actress Yao Chen's case—and some have, like their US peers, come badly unstuck. But in one respect they have trumped the celebrities of the west: monetising their lives.

"More than any other country, [KOLs] have taken the lead to be a true media vehicle," says Greg Paull, principal of R3, a global marketing consultancy. "Much like you would use a TV campaign or other promotion, most marketers in China have a KOL strategy."

Makers of everything from shampoo and chocolate such as Unilever, to purveyors of designer handbags including Burberry and Gucci, have swarmed to these influencers as a way to advertise their goods.

That has resulted in some unusual bedfellows. Watchmaker Jaeger-LeCoultre saw its brand awareness, as measured by the Baidu Index, more than double, after running a campaign with girl-next-door vlogger Papi Jiang. Actor Kris Wu has boosted sales for designers Bulgari and Burberry.

The two are among the teen idols being enlisted by luxury brands such as Longines and Tiffany to woo younger shoppers.

As multinationals latch on to KOLs as a means of selling goods to aspirational Chinese consumers, the paychecks they command are rising, according to ad agencies. Jaeger-LeCoultre paid "at least" RMB5m ($731,000) for Ms Jiang's 30-second video, estimates Kevin Gentle of Madjor, a digital branding agency.

But the results also can be big. Actress Yang Mi shared her birthday party, thrown by designer Michael Kors in a New York hotel, with her 72m followers on microblogging and livestreaming site Weibo—generating more than 12m comments and likes, according to digital agency L2.

In a uniquely Chinese twist, an entire industry profiting from the KOLs' ascent has sprung up. While YouTubers in the west are also paid to munch Oreo cookies on video or wear a designer's clothes, KOLs in China also pull in their own funds directly.

On top of advertising dollars, they make money from fans who can send virtual gifts and cash online, as well as paid endorsements and sponsorships—such as jeweller De Beers, which sponsored the wedding of celeb couple Liu Shishi and Wu Qilong.

At the top of the ladder, some KOLs even become investment vehicles in themselves: Ms Jiang, before China's regulators took issue with her swearing, raised just shy of $2m from venture capital investment into her company. SNH48, a funky girl band as well known for engaging with fans online as for their fishnet tights and distressed shorts, helped secure a $150m investment for their media group, Star48 Culture and Media Group, last month.

The KOL economy was estimated at Rmb58bn by CBNData in 2015—equivalent to more than that year's gross box-office receipts. Consultancy Analysis projects revenues will reach Rmb100bn next year.

Microbloggers on Weibo—which has overtaken US peer Twitter, which is blocked in China, in terms of both market capitalisation and subscriber numbers—had pulled in $1.7bn by October last year, according to Xinhua.

The KOLs owe their rise to the flourishing livestreaming industry, much as YouTube buoyed its screen celebrities. But a shift to short-form videos has breathed new life into the industry—especially for advertisers who produce their own content, such as behind-the-scenes footage of fashion shows.

Like YouTube, China's tech trinity of Baidu, Alibaba and Tencent all have video streaming platforms. But it is those targeting shorter-form video, such as Weibo, dating app and livestreaming player Momo, and social platform YY, that are attracting the most attention from advertisers.

Livestreaming periodically falls foul of the regulators—as highlighted by Beijing's recent crackdown on inappropriate content. Last week, new rules prompted technology and media companies such as Sina Weibo and Tencent to close down 291 video-streaming platforms and fire almost 10,000 journalists.

But the industry has been growing fast. There are more than 200 livestreaming apps, according to market research consultancy Frost & Sullivan, with over 200m registered users.

When it comes to livestreaming "a lot of platforms have a greater level of interactivity between the KOL and the watcher", says Brian Buchwald, cofounder and chief executive of consumer research company Bomoda. "They encourage live engagement... with the KOLs."

Viewers, however, tend to be platform-neutral, says Joe Ngai, managing partner of McKinsey China: "They follow the person, not the platform."

"We have clients who move all of their advertising online and KOL endorsement is the primary driver outside of Baidu search," says Mr. Buchwald. "They are trying to put as much money into KOLs as they can."

References 参考文献

BBC Storyworks. 2021. To the people, food is heaven. 01-25. From BBC website.

Brown, W. 2018. *Off the Wall: How We Feel About China*. Beijing: Foreign Languages Press.

Campbell, D. 2012. Expat interviews: Keeping sane in Shanghai. 04-13. From Expat Info Desk website.

Cao, C. 2019. New round of math teacher exchange draws record number of UK educators. 11-12. From *People's Daily* website.

Clark, D. 2016. *Alibaba: The House That Jack Ma Built*. New York: Harpers Collins.

Cui, F. D. 2021. Stranded whales saved in East China in dramatic rescue by officers and fishermen, broadcast live online. 07-07. From *Global Times* website.

Expat Info Desk. 2018. A thriving metropolis where east meets west. From Expat Info Desk website.

Hong, Y. 2020. American professor tells wonderful stories of China to the world. 01-21. From *People's Daily* website.

Jack, A. 2020. China surpasses Western government African university scholarships. 06-23. From FT Chinese website.

Laboratorio dell'Espresso. 2019. The Chinese tea ceremony: A fascinating ritual. 11-20. From Laboratorio dell'Espresso website.

Li, Y. 2016. Chinese parents are always watching. 04-24. From *Global Times* website.

Liu, S. Y., & Martha, A. 2009. *The Inside Story Behind Jack Ma and the Creation of the World's Biggest Online Marketplace*. New York: Harpers Collins.

Liu, X. M. 2020. Shoulder your important missions and contribute your youth and talent. 06-11. From *China Daily* website.

Lucas, L. 2017. Brands turn to China's digital influencers to fuel sales. 07-03. From *Financial Times* website.

Qin, A. 2016. China's viral idol: A girl next door with fast-talking attitude. 08-25. From *New York Times* website.

Rao, T. 2020. The reclusive food celebrity Li Ziqi is my quarantine queen. 04-22. From *New York Times* website.

Tewari S. 2021. Elephants' 500 km-trek across China baffles scientists. 06-23. From BBC website.

The Economist. 2019. Weak tea doesn't sell. *The Economist*, 431 (9141): 56.

The Guardian. 2019. China challenges Hollywood with own sci-fi blockbuster. 02-11. From *The Guardian* website.

Thring, O. 2012. *A Bite of China*: The finest food TV ever? 09-12. From *The Guardian* website.

Wan, L. 2021. Biodiversity conservation in China has improved but more efforts are needed: Chinese conservationists. 05-24. From *Global Times* website.

Wang, Q. Y. 2014. Beijing approves "two children" policy. 02-21. From *China Daily* website.

Xinhua News Agency. 2016. President Xi urges new media outlet to tell China stories well. 12-31. From *Global Times* website.

Yuhas, A. 2020. Why *Star Wars* keeps bombing in China. 01-14. From *New York Times* website.

Zhao X. Y. 2017. Country's English language ranking improves. 11-09. From *China Daily* website.

Zou, S. 2020. Education cooperation to resume online. 12-23. From *China Daily* website.

邓肯·克拉克.2016.阿里巴巴：马云和他的102年梦想.李鑫译.北京：中信出版社.

凯茜.2017.过半中国夫妇仍然不想要二胎.1月9日.来自大耳朵英语网站.

潘威廉.2018.我不见外——来自老潘的中国来信.韦忠和译.北京：外文出版社.

趣读经济学人.2020.网课拉近师生关系.3月4日.来自知乎网站.

THU生活英语慕课.2019.矛盾的儒学.4月10日.来自搜狐网站.

特加尔·饶.2020.隐居一隅的美食博主，疫情期间的田园女王——李子柒.晋其角译.4月28日.来自纽约时报中文网.

苏珊·福沃德.2020.原生家庭如何修补自己的性格缺陷.黄姝译.北京：北京时代华文书局.

尤哈斯·艾伦.2020.《星球大战》在中国为何屡战屡败.晋其角、杜然译.1月15日.来自纽约时报中文网.

Appendix 1 Keys to Exercises

Unit 1

Text A

I True or False

1. F
2. T
3. T
4. T
5. T

II Reading Comprehension

1. The global challenges are how to seek medicines, vaccine, preventive technologies and testing methods that will help mankind beat COVID-19.
2. The three missions are the mission of promoting the progress of mankind, realizing national rejuvenation and deepening China-UK relationship.
3. Science and technology could provide new impetus for the prosperity in the world and play a bigger role in the progress of mankind.
4. Ambassador Liu expects young students to keep in mind this mission and seize the opportunities to take part in scientific and technological innovation, enhance exchanges and share outcomes.
5. The two countries are both great civilisations with numerous talents and profound culture. The British people have enormous enthusiasm to learn more about China and Chinese youth has strength to bridge the cultural gap, to tear down ideological fences, and to help extend the reach of China's stories and the stories of China-UK cooperation.

V Translation

习近平主席指出，中国国际电视台应该有文化自信、聚焦新闻、有观众意识，并使用融媒体。中国国际电视台应该讲好中国的真实故事，把中国的声音传播好，让世界看到一个多维多彩的中国，把中国呈现为世界和平的建设者、全球发展的贡献者、国际秩序的维护者；习近平主席指出，应努力构建命运共同体。中共中央政治局常委刘云山表示，中国国际电视台应承担起与世界接轨的责任。他指出，中国国际电视台应该把新闻内容放在第一位，突出以习近平同志为核心的国家治理新思想和新战略，讲述中国发展的故事，阐释中国的道路、理论和贡献，在重大的全球事务和国际问题上有发言权。

Text B

I True or False

1. T
2. F
3. T
4. T
5. T

II Reading Comprehension

1. South Africa, Russia, German, French and other European countries and NGOs such as ABSA and the MasterCard Foundation.
2. China can be expected to keep increasing scholarships for African students for many years to come.
3. Long-term continuity means the long and sustainable support of Chinese government for African students.
4. While scholarship providers typically track whether beneficiaries complete their courses, most share little information on criteria and frequently do not include verifiable metrics or have objectives to recruit those from disadvantaged backgrounds.
5. China's policy was to use soft power to build long-term influence, but its universities don't spend a lot of time keeping in touch with people who've been there, while Western universities make fundraising-linked efforts to cultivate alumni networks.

V Translation

几十年的经济发展使中国领导人得以实现教育现代化，并将中国转变为国际学生的枢纽。过去，外国学生只来中国学习语言课程，但现在越来越多的来自世界各地的学生被吸引到中国学习技术课程并获得专业学位。中国的经济繁荣也为中产阶级家庭送子女出国留学创造了新的机会。在中国领导人推动以受过良好教育的劳动力为动力的创新型经济之际，培养国内外人才将是至关重要的。

Unit 2

Text A

I True or False

1. T
2. T
3. F
4. T
5. T

II Reading Comprehension

1. Ma enjoyed Mark Twain's *The Adventures of Tom Sawyer* very much and relished any opportunity to practice his English. He started waking up before dawn and riding his bicycle for forty minutes to the Hangzhou Hotel to greet foreign tourists.

2. Ma maintained a pen pal relationship with the Morleys for a few years by writing to each other. Ma would correspond regularly with Ken, asking him to "double space his letters so that any corrections could be sent back in the spaces". David recalled that the original with corrections was returned for learning purposes with the reply letter.

3. A barrow boy is a man or boy who sells fruits or other goods from a barrow in the street. Here the author suggests Ma rose up from nobody.

4. English helps Ma understand the world better, meet the best CEOs and leaders in the world, and understand the distance between China and the world.

5. With rich knowledge of the history of the area, and a knack for storytelling, Jack embraced the opportunity to show more foreign tourists around the sights of West Lake.

V Translation

马云于 1964 年 9 月 10 日出生于杭州西湖畔的一个家庭。"马云传奇"中有种说法是，他的家庭是普通而平凡的，但普通的家庭并不会住在西湖岸边。马云的父母一生都是评弹的专业表演者。评弹是中国南方苏州的一种传统的评书和民谣演唱形式。

基于这样的背景，马云自小就和父母讲苏州话长大，他对这座城市和这里历史悠

久的传统有着强烈的依恋。俗话说，苏州有两种人：一种人爱说，一种人爱听。要找出马云即席演讲和激发高效惊人能力源自哪里，我们不必过于深入了解他的背景。从小到大，马云都在观摩和学习专业演讲，尤其是他父母的演讲。他的演讲风格可能归因于他早期的经历：用简单直接的语言准确解释他的意思。他不说一句废话便能直击主题。

Text B

I True or False

1. F
2. F
3. T
4. T
5. F

II Reading Comprehension

1. Because the author heard of Robin, a junior in International Business and Economics who seemed to know everyone and be involved in everything, and had won numerous scholarships and awards. He believed that Robin had the ability and stamina to help him beat the deadline.

2. When she was in her family way, her water broke. After she was sent to the hospital, the doctor recommended a C-section which was quite dangerous at that time.

3. Robin was named in Chinese homophone "Fei Fei", meaning "to fly".

4. Robin quickly gained attention and respect from teachers and students alike as she became top in her class—even becoming a tutor for older children.

5. She gave that privilege to the No. 2 student when she applied for a master's degree at Harvard.

V Translation

　　我永远不会忘记当收到中国驻瑞典大使馆的电话通知我获得这一殊荣时，我是多么的兴奋。这是我一生中最棒的时刻之一。获此殊荣意味着我在博士研究期间的科学研究发展和成就从专业的角度受到了中国政府的高度认可。因此，我为获得此项奖励感到非常自豪和荣幸。最重要的是，我衷心感谢我的导师 Erik Renström 教授和我的联合导师张恩明副教授，他们在我的整个博士学习历程中，给予了我巨大的鼓励、帮助、支持和指导。如若没有他们的指导，我永远不会获得这个奖项。我还要感谢隆德大学为我提供了一个发展自我的绝佳平台。

Unit 3

Text A

I True or False

1. F
2. T
3. F
4. F
5. T

II Reading Comprehension

1. Local public security, fire, fishery and other departments and nearby enthusiastic fishermen.
2. Rescuers worked together to get the whales onto stretchers and move them to a dug-out puddle, another wave of rescuers continued to spray them with water and used wet towels to prevent the water from evaporating. The rescue brigade also brought in ice to cool the whales down.
3. Predation into unfamiliar waters, changes in seawater tides, neurological diseases, and malfunctioning navigation systems.
4. Releasing the whales back into the sea as soon as possible after treatment of their injuries and illnesses.
5. Because of overfishing, offshore pollution and busy shipping lanes.

V Translation

　　孙全辉建议，除了及时救助搁浅鲸鱼外，还应全面加强海洋生态保护，包括增加海洋保护区数量，严格执行海洋休禁渔政策。为保护鱿鱼资源，中国渔政部门要求从7月1日起开始暂停中国渔民在公海部分海域进行捕鱼。7月1日至9月30日，除了部分国家专属经济区以外的大西洋西南部的公海部分海域将实行休渔。从9月1日到11月30日，东太平洋公海部分海域将实行休渔。

Text B

I True or False

1. F
2. T
3. F
4. T
5. F

II Reading Comprehension

1. It's believed that the elephants started their journey in the spring of 2020 from Xishuangbanna National Nature Reserve in the southwest of China.

2. Elephants are matriarchal with the oldest and wisest female leading the group of grandmothers, mothers and aunties along with their sons and daughters.

3. Because elephants are very habitual and very routine driven, it's unusual for them to move to new areas when they're about to give birth.

4. Because elephants are so big, that if there is any sort of threat it takes too long for them to get up and lying down puts a lot of pressure on their heart and lungs.

5. Because elephants aren't evolved to be told what to do. If they are told what to do over long distances, it can create lots of aggressive behaviours.

V Translation

　　科学家们一致认为这次的象群移动不是迁徙，因为它不遵循固定路线。由于大量的保护措施，中国成为了世界上为数不多的大象数量在不断增长的地方之一。在中国对偷猎行为的严厉打击下，云南省的野生大象数量从20世纪90年代的193头增加到今天的300头左右。但是专家表示城市化和森林砍伐还是导致大象栖息地在不断减少，它们可能正在寻找一个更容易获得食物的新家。

Unit 4

Text A

I True or False

1. T
2. F

Appendix 1 Keys to Exercises

3. F
4. T
5. T

II Reading Comprehension

1. Wading out into the bog, finding a root, working out which direction it's lying in, then digging it out slowly and carefully by hand.

2. It captures ways of life that are evaporating in modern China.

3. Preserving by salt, pickling or wind, staple foods, the "gifts of nature" or "our rural heritage".

4. By using examples from across the country with shifting perspectives.

5. *A Bite of China* never patronises its subjects or viewers.

V Translation

人物总是其中最有趣的部分：一位在人迹罕至的山腰寻找松茸的老婆婆；一户在小兴安岭山麓制作韩国泡菜的家庭；一个捕梭鱼为晚饭的渔夫；一个上海女子在浴缸中放满活蟹，用白酒腌制，然后将醉蟹密封保存在陶器中。尽管根据节目介绍，很多出现在节目中的人物生活很艰难，比较贫穷，但节目以惊人的敏锐捕捉到了现代中国正在逐渐消失的生活方式。

Text B

I True or False

1. T
2. T
3. F
4. T
5. F

II Reading Comprehension

1. Mountain ranges and rivers, rainforests, grassland, deserts and coast.

2. *shaomai* dumplings, steamers of "phoenix claws" (aka chicken feet), sweet custard tarts and other delicate treats.

127

3. Fish sounds like the word for "surplus"; dumplings are prepared and wrapped communally, which promise wealth and good fortune by their resemblance to old silver ingots.
4. Chongqing hotpot is wickedly spicy, while Beijing-style *shuan yang rou* is more austere.
5. Because of the universal use of chopsticks and seasonings such as soy sauce.

V Translation

中国有句俗语："民以食为天。"尽管这句话源自大约 2000 年前汉代的一篇古文，但今天它比以往任何时候都更加真实可信。过去半个世纪中国的变化速度令人慨叹，但不变的是中国与食物的文化关联。与过去相比，尽管如今的中国城市可能看起来已经完全不同，但在农产品、产地和菜肴形式这些方面，中华食物古老的特征依然生生不息。在瞬息万变的中国，食物是文化认同感最重要的支柱之一。对食物的热爱、欣赏和理解定义了一个中国人的特质，无论未来发生什么，这一点都不会改变。如今，在全球各地都能享用到中餐，但若要真正理解中餐的文化内涵，感受其种类的万千变化，还是只有在中国亲自品鉴才行。

Unit 5

Text A

I True or False

1. F
2. T
3. F
4. F
5. F

II Reading Comprehension

1. Because Mr. Lin has caught his son being distracted by online games. He wants his son to know that he will inspect the browser for evidence of such naughtiness.
2. If connections are too wobbly for video calls, students can download audio files and assignments.
3. In poor rural areas, where some households lack Internet access, instruction by television fills the void. Students can watch TV.
4. The disruption is felt most keenly by pupils in the final year of secondary school.

Appendix 1 Keys to Exercises

5. The teacher-student relationship will become "less hierarchical", he predicts. That is because China's prolonged experiment with online learning is reducing the typical reserve between instructor and pupil. Teachers who were previously reluctant to give out their contact details on WeChat, a messaging app, now rely on it to respond to students' queries. At Mr. Yue's school, students may even call their teachers to ask for feedback.

V Translation

一位高级教育官员周二表示，在采取严格的疫情防控措施后，中国将恢复国际教育合作。教育部国际合作与交流司司长刘进表示，随着新冠肺炎疫情在全球蔓延，教育部将开展网络教育合作。刘志军在北京举行的新闻发布会上表示，在"十四五"规划期间（2021—2025年），我国将在海南省、粤港澳大湾区、长三角地区和雄安新区等地区推进国际教育合作上取得新突破。她表示，中国还将继续鼓励学生出国留学，以培养具有国际竞争力的人才，为中国的发展作出贡献；同时提高在中国留学的国际学生的教育质量。

Text B

I True or False

1. T
2. F
3. F
4. T
5. F

II Reading Comprehension

1. The life of a teacher in a Shanghai primary school differs quite a bit from that of teachers in most other countries. For one thing each teacher specialises in a particular subject—if you teach maths, you teach only maths. There are other differences too. School days are longer—from 07:00 until 16:00 or 17:00. Class sizes are larger. And lessons are shorter—each is 35 minutes long, followed by 15 minutes of unstructured play.

2. Covering less and making smaller incremental movements forward, ensuring the class move together as one and that you go over stuff again and again until it's truly understood.

3. This is one of the key attractions of the system—it helps poor children realise their potential, increasing social mobility.

4. The idea there is that effort brings rewards and so you will get this totally driven sort of idea but what you don't get is this creative problem-solving that requires space and mulling and dwelling. Another criticism of the system is that parents work children too hard. An estimated 80% of students receive private lessons outside school.

5. The fundamentals of this policy are right and it's incredibly inspiring to think everybody can become more freed up by maths.

V Translation

在过去十年里，上海的数学教学方法获得了世界各地的认可，因为它帮助上海在经济合作与发展组织的国际学生评估项目中，在2009年和2012年的十五六岁学生的数学成绩排名中名列前茅。在此期间，英国政府也在寻找不同的方法来提升本国的数学知识，最终决定在当地课程中采用上海数学教学的一些元素。

Unit 6

Text A

I True or False

1. T
2. T
3. F
4. T
5. T

II Reading Comprehension

1. The father is a nagging crank who expects his two adult sons to bankroll his lavish tastes. This leads to constant bickering between the brothers, neither of whom wants to be called "unfilial".

2. The daughter holds a grudge against her father (the two are pictured), and especially against her late mother, for having mistreated her while pampering her brothers. As a child she was made to wash her brothers' clothes. Her parents turned a blind eye when one of her brothers beat her.

3. For many female viewers born before 1979, when China introduced a one-child-per-couple policy (changed to two in 2016), such scenes have brought back painful memories.

4. Many people say the best measure of adherence to this virtue is whether a son takes good care of his parents in old age.

5. Because he throws tantrums and insists that his eldest son buy him a three-bedroom apartment (the son grudgingly does so). Commentators on social media have taken to calling the father a juying ("giant baby")—a characteristic common among parents in real life, they say. The Su children do their duty, but the audience is supposed to applaud the resentment they express.

V Translation

但最引起热议的是该剧对孝道的批判。即使在今天，对父母尽孝的儒家思想仍然是备受尊崇的。许多人认为，衡量一个人是否坚守这一美德最好的方法就是看他能否在父母年迈时照顾好他们。今日头条（一款中国新闻应用）最近开展的一项调查显示，中国有54%的老年人一半以上的支出由其成年子女们承担。毫无疑问，这在一定程度上是由于养老金体系不够完善所致。但来自北京的一位《都挺好》的粉丝表示，这也反映了一种"永远不要对父母说不"的文化。

Text B

I True or False

1. T
2. F
3. F
4. F
5. T

II Reading Comprehension

1. The country faces a new demographic issue: it looks set to become old before it becomes rich.

2. The key factors for most parents when considering a second child are the quality of schools, baby products, living environment and access to medical facilities. Other major considerations included whether a later pregnancy would be safe for the mother, if the family could even afford another child, and child care prior to kindergarten.

3. Different provinces have set the wheels in motion to support women who want to have a second child, with plans in the pipeline to offer them longer paid maternal leave.

4. Because in developed countries, where women have the opportunity of education level and salaries on par with or near to their male counterparts, young people's lifestyles—and their interest in marrying or having children—have radically shifted.

5. In order to avoid a "low birth rate trap", China will continue to observe its demographic data and will take measures to intervene should it need to further relax its family planning policy.

V Translation

2016年11月下旬，中国社会科学院发布了《中国人口与劳动报告》，显示二孩政策并不是计划生育改革的"终点"。为了避免"低出生率陷阱"，中国将继续观察其人口数据，一旦需要进一步放宽计划生育政策，将采取干预措施。最近的计划生育政策改革，如果说有什么区别的话，那就是标志着一个新时代的诞生。

Unit 7

Text A

I True or False

1. F
2. F
3. T
4. F
5. T

II Reading Comprehension

1. The "weak tea" refers to the blandly globalized movies which are trying to enter a foreign film market.

2. The audiences in different countries have distinguished tastes.

3. Domestic films.

4. Because of the cultural gap. The Western reviewers have been used to movies involving Western heroes saving the world.

5. According to Lu Jingshan, it is no mean feat for Western films to enter Chinese market. Cultural gaps, audiences tastes and domestic films' dominance are the main obstacles.

Appendix 1 Keys to Exercises

V Translation

多年来，好莱坞制片人们斥巨资打造了一系列影片，并认为美国观众和中国观众没有太大不同，都会为同一部精心打造的全球化电影欢笑、哭泣和欢呼。然而，中国电影市场总是证明他们错了。《复仇者联盟》系列电影在中国拥有庞大而独特的粉丝群体，他们总说喜欢这个系列电影的缘由正是他们认同与所处环境格格不入的英雄们，在一个残酷、批判的世界中挣扎前行。

Text B

I True or False

1. T
2. F
3. F
4. F
5. T

II Reading Comprehension

1. The *Star Wars* is one of the most successful franchises in history which is highly influential among several generations of Western audiences.
2. Chinese audiences have grown up with Marvel's comic-book heroes.
3. Michael Berry holds that almost no one in China grew up with the original *Star Wars*.
4. Ying Xiao thinks that China's box office has recently been dominated by homegrown competitors.
5. *Star Wars* is not deeply rooted in China.

V Translation

尽管迪士尼积极地努力推广《星球大战》，但该系列在中国的收益仍在不断减少。公司用上了迷你帝国冲锋队员和实物大小的星际战机，并与中国合作伙伴在一系列项目上展开合作，包括翻译相关书籍，制作一个中韩男子组合的音乐视频。

这样的行为突显出在中国电影市场赚钱有多么重要。中国目前已是全球第二大电影市场。最新的《复仇者联盟》系列电影在中国的票房收入超过 5 亿美元，《变形金刚》和《速度与激情》等系列电影的票房收入持续达到数亿美元。

Unit 8

Text A

I True or False

1. F
2. T
3. T
4. T
5. F

II Reading Comprehension

1. Her digitally altered voice, rapid-fire delivery, jump cuts and urbanites related themes.
2. The subjects in her videos, like cheating boyfriends, celebrity culture and regional dialects, are very familiar to educated young urbanites.
3. With the support from the venture capital, Papi Jiang could start her own business.
4. Attracting fans and then monetizing this attraction.
5. It seemed that the foul language did not diminish her appeal.

V Translation

具有官方背景的中国互联网信息中心于本月发布的一份报告显示，中国的网络已经越来越多地由移动端驱动，在 7.1 亿中国网民中，超过 92% 的人使用手机上网。他们在网上购物，交友聊天，在微博和微信等应用中获取资讯，进行娱乐。

Text B

I True or False

1. T
2. T
3. F
4. F
5. T

Appendix 1 Keys to Exercises

Ⅱ Reading Comprehension

1. D.I.Y. pastoral lifestyle.
2. For them, Ms. Li's videos become a reliable source of escape and comfort.
3. The country lifestyle.
4. The industrial supply chains would be severely affected by the pandemic.
5. Open question.

Ⅴ Translation

就像某些末世后小说中的主人公一样，李子柒几乎总是一个人，不过她似乎并不孤独，她骑马穿过野花丛中，或者提着一篮一篮的红薯站在橘花树下。她似乎不知疲倦，专注，自信，独立。

这些视频让人深感慰藉。但是不仅如此——它们揭示了每道菜所有组成部分中倾注的复杂而密集的劳动，同时也让漫长而孤独的生产过程显得有意义和有价值。

Appendix 2 Suggested Translation

Unit 1

Text A

勇担时代重任，贡献青春才华

——刘晓明大使在 2019 年度"国家优秀自费留学生奖学金"颁奖仪式上的讲话
2020 年 6 月 10 日，中国驻英国大使馆

老师们、同学们：

  大家上午好！

  很高兴出席"2019 年度国家优秀自费留学生奖学金"颁奖仪式。首先，我谨代表中国驻英国大使馆和驻曼彻斯特、爱丁堡、贝尔法斯特总领馆，向全英 47 名获奖同学表示热烈祝贺！同时，也向获奖同学的导师们表示衷心感谢！

  我担任驻英大使以来，每年都坚持参加这个活动，今年是第 11 个年头，也是一个非常特殊的年份。因为新冠肺炎疫情的原因，我们第一次采用视频连线的形式颁奖。

  这场突如其来的疫情，改变的不只是我们的交流方式，也给人类社会带来严峻挑战、给世界经济带来巨大冲击、给国际格局带来深远影响。这让我们更加体会到，人类命运与前途休戚与共，人类命运共同体理念的弥足珍贵。可以说，人类社会的发展进步、中华民族的伟大复兴、中英关系的行稳致远都比以往任何时候更需要人才和担当。在此背景下，今天的颁奖活动更具有特殊意义。我希望大家牢记三个使命：

  一是推动人类进步的使命。习近平主席在前不久给中国科技工作者代表回信中指出，"创新是引领发展的第一动力，科技是战胜困难的有力武器"。解决全球性挑战、推动人类不断进步，始终是科技创新的重要使命。人类战胜新冠肺炎疫情的希望，在于科技创新。我们都期盼全世界科学家加快药物、疫苗、防疫、检测等方面的科研攻关，力争早日取得惠及全人类的突破性成果。人类实现合作共赢与永续发展，也在于科技创新。希望大家牢记创新使命，抓住创新机遇，推进科技创新，促进科技交流和成果共享，让科技发挥最大效应，为实现各国经济社会繁荣提供新助力，为推动人类进步发挥更大作用。

  二是推动民族复兴的使命。爱国主义是中华民族的民族心、民族魂。报效祖国是各种志向的底盘，也是人生的脊梁。中华人民共和国成立 70 多年来，我们实现了从

站起来、富起来到强起来的伟大飞跃，开启了全面建设社会主义现代化强国的新征程。今年是我们全面建成小康社会，消除绝对贫困，决胜第一个百年奋斗目标的历史性时刻。青年一代有理想、有本领、有担当，国家就有前途，民族就有希望。实现中华民族伟大复兴的中国梦，离不开一代代青年的接力奋斗。希望大家弘扬留学报国的光荣传统，把人生理想融入实现中华民族伟大复兴中国梦的奋斗中，把学到的本领奉献给祖国和人民，让青春之光闪耀在为梦想奋斗的道路上。

三是推动中英友好的使命。自中国国家留学基金委设立国家优秀自费留学生奖学金以来，迄今已有来自约 70 所英国高校的 509 名优秀学子获此殊荣。无论你们今后身在何处，作为 22 万在英中国留学生的优秀代表，希望大家为中英两国学术、教育、科技、商业等各领域交流合作作出贡献。2017 年，在驻英使馆的支持下，历届获得"优自奖"的留英学子自发组织成立了全球首个"优自奖"联谊会。今年初，国内疫情爆发时，联谊会第一时间组织募捐，购买医疗物资驰援湖北；在英国疫情爆发后，联谊会又积极配合使馆组织医学专家多次举办在线防疫知识讲座、在线问诊等活动，帮助广大学生学者安心留在英国继续学习、工作。大家用实实在在的爱心和善举，架起了中英"交融互助之桥"。

中英两国社会制度、历史文化和发展阶段不同，但都是人文精英荟萃、文化积淀深厚的伟大国家，也是东西方文明的重要代表。在英国工作生活 10 多年里，我深感英国民众对了解中国有着巨大热情，但也时常不得不应对一些政客和媒体的偏见和歪曲。讲好中国故事、传递好中国声音依然任重道远。希望大家发挥学贯中西的优势，努力跨越文化差异的鸿沟，打破意识形态的藩篱，讲好中国故事和中英合作故事。

习近平主席说，"有多大担当才能干多大事业，尽多大责任才能有多大成就"。希望大家心怀祖国、放眼世界，勇担重任、勇攀高峰，追求真理、锐意进取，为促进中外友好合作、为构建人类命运共同体贡献青春才华！

谢谢！

Text B

中国政府为非洲学生提供的大学奖学金名额超西方

中国政府向非洲学生提供的大学奖学金数量超过了西方主要国家政府的总和，表明中国在进行经济投资的同时也在运用"软实力"。

联合国教科文组织（UNESCO）发布的年度《全球教育监测报告》（*Global Education Monitoring Report*）显示，中国将在未来一学年向非洲学生提供 1.2 万个奖学金名额，主要用于支持他们在中国大学学习。

根据新型冠状病毒大流行前收集的数据，南非和俄罗斯也会向非洲学生提供数千个奖学金名额，而印度和土耳其提供的奖学金数量也在不断增加。

英国政府为非洲学生提供约 1100 个年度奖学金名额，主要是通过"志奋领奖学金项目"（Chevening Scholarship）。德国和法国政府各提供约 600 个，欧盟相关项目提供逾 300 个。其他欧洲和西方政府提供的支持较小。

牛津大学高等教育教授西蒙·马金森（Simon Marginson）表示，这一趋势反映了中国"一带一路"（Belt and Road）倡议相关的"软外交"努力，中国在该倡议下向包括非洲在内的世界各地的基础设施项目投入了大量资金。他说："中国的援助是地区性的，往往依据'一带一路'来确定。与英国相比，中国政策的特点之一是长期连续性。"他表示在英国有种倾向，"政策会随着不同的预算而发生变化，如果政府换届，这种倾向会更明显。但中国有望在未来很多年继续增加对非洲学生的奖学金。"

英国、法国、德国和其他西方捐助国往往将大部分教育援助预算集中在针对学龄儿童的支持项目上。联合国教科文组织的数据涵盖官方的由政府支持的奖学金项目，不包含各大学提供的支持。两家有企业背景的奖学金提供者也在大力支持非洲学生。南非联合银行（ABSA）和支付集团万事达卡（MasterCard）旗下慈善机构万事达基金会（MasterCard Foundation）都在大学奖学金的主要提供者之列。

联合国教科文组织的分析报告中强调，大多数奖学金被用于支持资助国的大学名额，而不是为学生提供非洲大学的名额，若用于后者将有助于加强这些机构。报告中还强调，虽然奖学金提供者通常会追踪受助者是否完成了学业，但它们大多很少分享有关申请条件的信息，而且往往不包括可验证的标准，也没有关于招收弱势背景的学生的目标。为了解决这一问题，观察人士呼吁修改奖学金制度，以增强非洲优秀学生的社会流动性，并发展非洲大陆自己的教育体系。

支持非洲大陆高等教育的慈善机构非洲撒哈拉教育（Education Sub-Saharan Africa）帮助分析了这些数据，该组织的主席帕特里克·邓恩（Patrick Dunne）表示："人们对奖学金的看法需要改变。我们可以让钱花得更值。如果更多地把关注点放在其影响上，就会有更多资金流入奖学金，我们就能看到回报。"

他呼吁建立一个更系统的奖学金体系，让最需要且符合资格的学生获得奖学金，让他们能获得更好的教育机会。

爱丁堡大学荣休教授肯尼斯·金（Kenneth King）强调，尽管中国的政策是利用软实力打造长期影响力，但中国的大学"没有花很多时间与去过中国求学的人保持联系"。他将中国的做法与西方大学进行了对比，努力培育校友网络是西方大学重要的筹资举措。

Unit 2

Text A

街头小贩

1964年9月10日，马云出生在上海西南百里外的杭州。父母给他取名为"云"，意思是"高高的白云"。他的姓"马"与汉语中的动物"马"是同一个字。

马云小时候就很喜欢英语及英文著作，特别喜欢听收音机中电台朗读的马克·吐温所著的《汤姆·索亚历险记》。后来，正是来到中国的外国游客让马云开始了解外面的世界。1978年年末，马云14岁时，中国实行改革开放政策，国家开始大力吸引外资，积极开展对外贸易。历经10年浩劫的中国国民经济濒临崩溃，极度需要硬通货。

1978年，杭州只接待了728名外国游客，但第二年就猛增到了4万多人。马云不放过任何练习英文的机会。常常是天刚破晓，他就起床，骑上自行车，花40分钟赶到杭州饭店去和外国游客攀谈。后来他回忆道："每天早晨从5点开始，我就在宾馆前读英语。很多游客来自美国，也有一些是欧洲人。我免费带他们游览西湖，他们教我英语。整整9年！我每天早晨都在练英语，不管天气好坏。"

马云的英文名字Jack是一位美国游客帮他起的。那位女游客的父亲和丈夫都叫Jack，所以她建议马云也用这个名字。他自认当时的英文水平不怎么样："只是能让人懂而已，但语法真是一团糟。"但马云一直认为学习英语给他的人生带来了巨大的帮助："英语帮了我大忙。它让我更好地了解这个世界，让我遇到了一些非常优秀的CEO和领导者，也让我认识到了中国和世界的差距。"

1980年，在杭州的外国游客中有这么一家人，他们是来自澳大利亚的莫利一家。父亲肯·莫利（Ken Morley）是一位电气工程师，刚刚退休，母亲叫朱迪，他们还有三个孩子：戴维、斯蒂芬和苏珊。当年，他们报名参加了由澳中友好协会组织的中国旅游。那是他们的第一次海外旅行。而对于马云，这家人的杭州之行则改变了他的生活。

如今，戴维在澳大利亚经营着一家瑜伽会馆。我费了一番周折，终于找到了他。他愉快地回忆起了那些往事，还把那次中国之行的照片拿给我看。从他口中，我才了解到多年以来他们一家人与马云之间形成的亲密无间的友谊。

1980年7月1日，莫利一家所在的澳大利亚旅行团从北京乘机飞抵杭州，然后乘大巴来到西湖边上的香格里拉酒店，也就是8年前尼克松总统及其随从曾下榻的杭州饭店。回忆起当年参观美国第一家庭曾入住的套房（当时他们旅行团的领队住了那间房）时，戴维说道："我们三个小孩都被那里的马桶座圈给迷住了，那是用奢华的红色天鹅绒做的。"

澳大利亚旅行团第二天的行程安排是，先乘船游览西湖，然后顺便参观西湖旁的茶园及六和塔，最后返回饭店，下午6点半用晚餐。趁着晚上自由活动的时间，戴维和旅行中结识的一个女孩凯娃（Keva）一起溜出宾馆，沿着路一直走到了宾馆对面可俯瞰西湖的孤山公园。除了在园子里闲逛，俩人还玩起一种弹火柴的游戏。这是凯娃教给戴维的一种游戏，要把火柴头朝下竖立在火柴盒磷面上，然后用手指轻弹火柴，看着它旋转着飞出去，然后……按戴维的原话说就是"可能会太平无事"。幸运的是，那天公园并未因此失火。但他们俩的古怪行为却引起了一位 15 岁少年的注意，这就是马云。

戴维回忆道："晚上自由活动的时候，我们在公园里玩火柴，一个男孩儿走过来和我们打招呼，他想锻炼一下自己新学的英语口语技能。他介绍了自己，我们互相寒暄了几句，约定之后再来这个公园碰面。"

旅行团在杭州一直待到了 7 月 4 日，那天戴维与妹妹苏珊在公园里和马云以及几个本地孩子一起玩飞盘。戴维给我描述了当时的情景：他们把鞋子和其他东西摆在地上，划定好比赛场地，比赛"一下子引来了几百个中国人看热闹"。马云的父亲马来法还在他们游戏时照了相。

戴维的父亲肯·莫利说他第一次见到马云时，还以为他是"货郎"，或者说"街头小贩"。"他非常想练习自己的英语，又很友善，我的几个孩子们都被他打动了。"

他们家与马云后来一直保持着联系，戴维说："杭州一别后，我和他就成了笔友，一直就靠写信联系。这样过了几年后，我爸爸打算帮助一下这个男孩了。"马云还定期与肯通信，称他为"父亲"，肯让马云"把字距留大点，这样好在回信时把一些纠正写在字距空白处"。戴维解释道："最初是想通过这些纠正让马云来学习英语。我觉得这对他非常有帮助，也鼓励了他继续学习英语"。

马云的英语水平在不断提高，加之熟知杭州风情和悠久历史，又善于讲故事，于是他就找机会带领越来越多的外国游客游览西湖景点。他特别喜欢去杭州的茶馆，当地人会在茶馆里下象棋、打牌，以及听"大书"。

马云经常陪着奶奶去寺里烧香拜佛。他着迷于太极，还非常喜欢读《水浒传》，书中 108 将的故事深深打动了他。阿里巴巴早期的一个目标就是凑足 108 位员工，这也与《水浒传》相关。

Text B

费菲——不曾是我的学生，却是最优秀的学生

亲爱的米奇叔叔、珍妮特：

在厦门问候你们！你们数次分享过在洛杉矶遇到的那些才华出众的中国学生，不过我觉得你们大概没有教过像费菲这样的学生。其实，她从来没当过我的学生，也没机会当我的学生了，因为她已经去哈佛大学修读硕士学位了。不过，我之前有机会同她合作撰写了一本书，那也是一次难忘的经历。

为了赶上厦大八十五周年校庆,我当时只有两个月的时间来撰写一本篇幅为363页的中英双语版《魅力厦大》。几位教授主动提出要帮忙,不过我之前听说了费菲,她是厦大国际经济与贸易系大三的学生,交际非常广泛,积极参与各项活动,也获得了不少奖学金和奖项。我思索着,如果校园里有人有这个能力和毅力帮我一起赶在交稿期限之前付梓,那就非费菲莫属了。当你耐心读完她的故事之后,就会理解为什么我说,她虽不曾是我的学生,却是最优秀的学生。

2005年,我在漳州校区的一场大型庆祝活动中第一次见到了费菲,那时她参与了活动的筹备工作。校园里的每一位外国人几乎都跟我提起过她。尽管她参加了许许多多活动,她的专业成绩年年名列第一。"不管我参加多少活动,学习始终是我的首要任务,"她说。了解到费菲的童年经历之后,我就可以理解为什么她这么重视学业。

某个酷热难当的夏天,费菲的母亲正在忙家务活,突然羊水破了。她的丈夫骑自行车赶了24公里路到达医院,一路上,即将生产的妻子在背后痛苦呻吟着。几个小时后到达医院,她非常痛苦,医生建议剖腹产。当时剖腹产手术风险极高,孕妇或胎儿(或两者同时)可能会有生命危险,因此,费菲的父亲不得不在多张表格和弃权声明上签字。幸好,母女平安,他将女儿取名为"费菲",寓意为"飞"(虽然是取谐音而不是字)。

费菲的父亲在中国一家大型的钢铁厂当工人,母亲在纺织厂工作。见到家里经济拮据,年幼的费菲便决定要想办法缓解家里的经济负担。她祖父教导她:"只要活着,就多学习,多做事。"于是她坚定地把接受教育当作迈向成功的道路。

起初,上学对费菲来说是孤独的。她最初腼腆内向,怯于交朋友,而且对自己寒酸的衣着打扮和简单粗糙的午饭感到难堪。不过,她的成绩名列前茅,很快就获得了老师和同学们的关注和尊重——甚至成了年纪比她大的孩子们的补习小老师。

如今,费菲在厦门大学的各方面表现都十分出色,一如既往保持着12年求学历程的那股劲头。她的英语发音像外国人一样标准,一口无可挑剔的普通话也让中国人惊叹不已,在中英文的各项比赛中赢得了不少奖项。她是厦大普通话协会会长,在厦大广播电台节目"英语咖啡屋"担任了两年的制作人兼播音员,还是厦大新闻中心的新闻节目主持人。费菲在《厦门日报》发表了几篇文章,曾代表厦大到北京参加"模拟联合国",而且曾在央视科教频道的节目《展望》上亮相。她主持过多场会议、宴会和比赛,曾与不同的国家的政府工作人员共事,收到过菲律宾政府的推荐信以及澳大利亚人由衷的感谢!

费菲平日的行程繁忙的令人敬畏,但尽管如此,她还是抽时间协助我在短短两个月内完成了长达363页的双语书籍。她收集考据资料,做访问,撰写多篇文章和多个章节,把英文翻译成中文,又把中文翻译成英文。

最触动我的不是她的职业道德,而是她正直的品格。作为班里的第一名,费菲有资格挑中国的任何一所大学读研究生,但她将这个权利让给了第二名的同学,她自己则专心申请哈佛大学的硕士。师长和同学纷纷说她不理智,"要是你没被录取怎么办?"

她解释说:"但是如果我不放弃名额,同时又被国外学校录取的话,第二名的同学要顶替我的名额就太迟了。这样做是对的。"对费菲、对哈佛大学来说都值得庆幸的是,她被录取了。不过,她出发去美国的时候,只带了100美元现金和两个装满书的行李箱,我问她:"只有100美元,你要怎么过?"

"我不需要钱,"费菲回答道,"我有全额奖学金和一笔生活津贴。"

我问费菲,她有什么生活目标,她说,短期内她的目标是让她父母有机会坐一趟飞机,教他们如何登机。假如有一天,费菲给她父母买来一辆飞机,我也不会觉得意外。飞吧,费菲,飞吧!

好了,米奇、珍妮特,这个月写到这儿差不多了。有空时写信给我们吧,我们的信箱都长蜘蛛网了。

比尔、苏、山农、马修,还有猫咪查理曼

2007年7月

Unit 3

Text A

华东地区搁浅的9头鲸鱼在政府和渔民的共同救援下脱困并全程进行网络直播

在当地官员、救援人员和附近居民争分夺秒的共同努力下,搁浅在华东海岸的12头瓜头鲸中有9头获救,数以百万计的网友通过网络直播见证了这一营救过程。

截止周三晚,获救鲸鱼中的8头已经被送返海洋,最后一头身体状况不佳的鲸鱼正继续接受观察和全面治疗。另外3头已死亡的鲸鱼尸体被放入冷冻库,将用于研究。

当地居民在周二上午8点左右向当局报告发现了搁浅鲸鱼,它们被困在距中国东部浙江省台州临海市海岸数百米的滩涂中。当地公安、消防、渔政等部门和附近热心渔民随即迅速展开了救援行动。

据救援人员反映,由于近来天气炎热,而且搁浅位置离海岸很远,救援极其困难。"这些鲸鱼有2米长又非常重,因此很难移动它们。"

救助鲸鱼的整个过程被媒体全程直播,数百万人观看了救援人员下海,对鲸鱼进行安置,并不断向鲸鱼泼水。

在救援人员齐心协力将鲸鱼抬上担架并把它们移到挖出的水坑后,另一波救援人员继续向它们泼水,并用湿毛巾盖住它们以减少水分蒸发。救援队还带来了冰块帮助鲸鱼降温。

"看到警察和公众齐心协力,迅速成功救援了这么大的动物,真的很受感动,"住在附近的一位王姓台州居民告诉《环球时报》。

世界动物保护协会科学家孙全辉对《环球时报》表示,虽然沿海地区经常发生鲸鱼搁浅事件,但一次搁浅 12 头的情况相对罕见。

此次鲸鱼搁浅的原因尚不清楚。"常见的原因包括进入陌生水域捕食、海水潮汐的变化、神经系统疾病和自身导航系统故障。人们普遍认为,人工声纳和疾病是鲸类导航能力受损的主要原因,"孙全辉说。

孙全辉指出,野生鲸鱼难以适应圈养,在得到救治后应尽快放归大海,这也是现场救援队的策略。

孙全辉还对鲸鱼的整体状况表示担忧。"救助搁浅鲸类的成功率往往不高。救助过程中可能会有一些生病或受伤的个体死亡,有的个体甚至在返回深水区后还会再次搁浅。"

本周早些时候,在中国南方广东省深圳市大鹏湾附近海域发现了另一种稀有鲸鱼。据深圳市大鹏新区综合办介绍,6 月 29 日发现一头被列为国家一级保护动物的布氏鲸出没于大鹏湾海域,并一直在该区域逗留。

当地官员成立了专门的工作小组来做好布氏鲸的保护工作,并呼吁过往船只不要围观,这一系列举措获得了众多网友的好评。

专家指出,中国海域连续出现鲸鱼可能表明鲸类生存环境发生了变化。

"布氏鲸已在深圳海域停留多日,并观察到其明显的觅食行为,说明该海域食物资源较为丰富,海洋环境可能更适合布氏鲸等海洋哺乳动物生存。"孙全辉告诉《环球时报》。

由于过度捕捞、近海污染和航道繁忙,过去活跃在中国近海的一些鲸类动物的生存曾受到很大影响,许多物种被列入最近更新的《国家重点保护野生动物名录》。

孙全辉建议,除了及时救助搁浅鲸鱼外,还应全面加强海洋生态保护,包括增加海洋保护区数量,严格执行海洋休禁渔政策。

为保护鱿鱼资源,中国渔政部门要求从 7 月 1 日起开始暂停中国渔民在公海部分海域进行捕鱼。7 月 1 日至 9 月 30 日,除了部分国家专属经济区以外的大西洋西南部的公海部分海域将实行休渔。从 9 月 1 日到 11 月 30 日,东太平洋公海部分海域将实行休渔。

Text B

中国象群长途跋涉 500 公里让科学家感到困惑

大象本质上是非常聪明的动物,经过日复一日的研究,专家已经对它们了如指掌。然而,中国的一群濒危大象让全球科学家都傻了眼,同时也吸引了全国的关注。

大象短距离的迁徙并不罕见。但一年多来，这一象群一直在中国境内长途跋涉。它们现已背井离乡，偏离原来的栖息地近500公里（310英里）。

据了解，该象群是去年春天从中国西南部、靠近缅甸和老挝边境的西双版纳国家级自然保护区出发的。它们一路北上，并在过去的几个月里路过了许多村庄、城镇和城市。

一路上人们看到象群损毁大门、"掠袭"商店、"偷盗"食物、在泥塘中嬉戏、在运河里洗澡、在森林中打盹。人们还看到象群把田里的作物一卷而空，还大摇大摆地进入居民的房子——有一次，它们成功地用象鼻打开了居民院里的水龙头，排队喝起了水。

现在人们认为它们又开始向南移动，最后一次发现它们是在玉溪市附近的时街乡。目前尚不清楚它们是否要返回故乡，也不知道它们为什么会进行这次漫长的旅途——这是中国已知最远的一次象群移动。接下来会发生什么，谁也说不准。

科学家的困惑

"事实是，没人知道为什么。这几乎肯定与象群对资源的需求有关——食物、水、栖息地——这有一定的道理，因为在有野生亚洲象生存的大多数区域，都存在人类干扰增加所导致的栖息地破碎化、流失和资源减少现象。"纽约城市大学亨特学院大象心理学助理教授约书亚·普洛特尼克告诉BBC。

普洛特尼克先生补充说，象群的迁移还可能与其社群形式有关。象群是母系社会，由其中最年长、聪明的雌象领导着一群祖母、母亲、姑母以及它们的儿女组成的群体。青春期后，雄象会离开象群单独行动或与其他雄象短时间地结伴而行。它们只会为了交配与雌象待在一起，在交配完后就会离开。

然而，这群由16或17头大象组成的象群在出发时包含了3头雄象。其中2头雄象在出发一个月后离群，剩下1只在本月早些时候离开了象群。

"这并不罕见，但我很惊讶它能呆这么久。这可能是因为身处陌生领域。我看到它们在走进一个城镇或村庄时，彼此走得很近——这是受到压力的表现。"西双版纳热带植物园教授兼首席研究员阿希姆萨·坎波斯·阿尔塞兹表示。

与其他哺乳动物相比，大象在行为上更接近人类，它们会感受到一系列不同情感，例如出生时的喜悦、死亡时的悲伤和身处异域的焦虑。

当其中2头雌象在旅途中分娩时，研究人员感到非常惊讶。总部设在赞比亚的野生动物保护组织"巡护员国际"的丽莎·奥利维尔向BBC表示："大象非常遵循自己的习惯和固有规律，而跑到陌生地区分娩是不寻常的，因为它们总是试图找到最安全的地方分娩。"

据奥利维尔女士表示，那些大象睡在一起的著名照片也很不寻常，"通常幼象睡在地上，成年大象则靠在树上或白蚁丘上。因为体型太大，在面临威胁时它们需要很长时间才能站起身，而躺下会给它们的心脏和肺部带来很大的压力。"

"躺着睡觉表明它们都非常劳累——可以说是筋疲力尽——这一切对它们来说显然是前所未有的。象群的大部分交流都是依赖次声波——通过感知脚部的振动——但在城镇和城市，它们听到更多的是车辆的声音。"

生存空间减少

科学家们一致认为这次的象群移动不是迁徙，因为它不遵循固定路线。

由于大量的保护措施，中国成为世界上为数不多的大象数量在不断增长的地方之一。在中国对偷猎行为的严厉打击下，云南省的野生大象数量从20世纪90年代的193头增加到今天的300头左右。

但是专家表示，城市化和森林砍伐还是导致大象栖息地在不断减少，它们可能正在寻找一个更容易获得食物的新家。

这些丛林巨兽是无情的进食机器，它们食量惊人，因此它们一生中的大部分时间都在寻找食物，每天需要150～200公斤的食物。

从空中围观

专家们很高兴这次的象群旅程没有出现任何与人类的危险对抗，此外还有其他一些积极的方面。

官方部署了无人机来监控象群，在不会惊扰到大象的情况下为研究人员提供了大量高质量信息，还给热切关注的公众奉上了大量令人难忘的照片。

奥利维尔女士还强调了中国政府、地方政府和保护组织在保护象群方面的密切合作。最近几个月，有关部门一直在放置食物诱饵并用卡车堵塞道路，引导大象转移到安全地带。

"我很高兴，这种方法不是很有侵扰性。一个非常常见的错误就是试图告诉大象它们应该做什么。大象还没有进化到可以被告知做什么。如果在漫长旅途中我们都试图告诉它们该做什么，会导致它们产生许多攻击性行为，"阿希姆萨·坎波斯·阿尔塞兹先生说。

中国媒体每天都在关注这群大象。它们俨然成为社交媒体的热点话题。所有的关注提升了国人对中国濒危象群处境的认知和敏感性，而这一事件引发的全球的兴趣可能会产生更加深远的影响。"这种关注和曝光有助于全世界的环境保护，"奥利维尔女士说。

<h1 style="text-align:center">Unit 4</h1>

Text A

《舌尖上的中国》——有史以来最好的美食节目？

每年秋天，中国湖北省内临近长江的湖泊水位开始下降，变成厚厚的沼泽，覆盖着一层腐殖质。每天都有100条左右的小船来到这里，在日出前昏暗的蓝灰色光线笼罩下，人们撑船划行在水位下降的河流中。他们正在寻找莲藕，这种富含淀粉的食物是亚洲烹饪的一大特色，经常出现在冬季的浓汤中，带来些许甜味。

我从来没有想过莲藕是从哪里来的。实际上采摘莲藕的过程是非常困难、肮脏和危险的。莲藕可能有一两米长，深深地埋在湖床粘稠的淤泥中。它们很脆，很容易被折断或划伤，而且没有机器可以把它们挖取出来。你只能走入漫过膝盖的沼泽，找到埋藏的莲藕，想办法确定它在淤泥中的走势，然后用手小心翼翼地挖出来。长达14小时的劳作结束后，挖藕人像士兵或橄榄球员一样彼此交流着身体酸痛、肌肉撕裂、脚踝扭伤和韧带扭曲。他们盼望着严寒的来临，因为这意味着更多的人会做莲藕汤，他们的产品价格就会上涨。

这仅仅是我所看过的最佳美食节目的一部分而已。我敢说这是有史以来最好的美食节目。《舌尖上的中国》于5月由中国中央电视台在中国播出。全国最著名的30位制片人历时一年多拍摄了7集50分钟的剧集。他们在全国各地进行了拍摄，北达东北的冰封湖泊，南至柳州的茂密竹林。

人物总是其中最有趣的部分：一位在人迹罕至的山腰寻找松茸的老婆婆；一户在小兴安岭山麓制作韩国泡菜的家庭；一个捕梭鱼为晚饭的渔夫；一个上海女子在浴缸中放满活蟹，用白酒腌制，然后将醉蟹密封保存在陶器中。尽管根据节目介绍，很多出现在节目中的人物生活很艰难，比较贫穷，但节目以惊人的敏锐视角捕捉到了现代中国正在逐渐消失的生活方式。

每一集都有一个主题：盐渍、腌制和风干、主食、"大自然的馈赠"或"我们的田野"。制作人用来自全国各地的例子来探索每一集的核心理念。视角的转换从宏观到微观：从直升机拍摄的霓虹都市或湖泊背后植被覆盖的山脉到一根穿透土层的竹笋。

《舌尖上的中国》计划在包括德国和美国在内的20个国家播出，但目前海外观众只能在YouTube上观看。业余的字幕翻译可能有些糟糕。（老人们非常享受美食："虽然他们的味蕾处于退化期，但他们依然记得家乡的美味。"）

但这个节目最让我喜爱的一点是它从不刻意迎合片中人物或取悦观众。制片人非常自信影片所呈现的内容足以吸引观众，所以全心全意地把成片尽可能地剪辑制作得令人着迷。严格来说，这不是一档烹饪节目，虽然我们经常在节目中看到有人在做饭，而且该节目还搭配有一本食谱（目前只有中文版在售）。相反，它具有一种更传统的、约翰·里斯式的教育意义。《舌尖上的中国》可能是相当于美食节目中的《人类的攀升》、克拉克爵士的《文明》或爱登堡的最佳作品。

英国美食节目也有过高光时刻，但从未尝试制作过这样的剧集。当你看了几集《舌尖上的中国》后，再回头去看自己国家的美食电视节目，发现只有苏菲·达儿和毛毛骑手的身影时，不可能不感到有些谦卑甚至惭愧。

Text B

民以食为天

中国是14亿美食爱好者的家园。这听上去似乎有点夸张,但在世界上人口最多的国家,饮食文化就是文化本身。无论你是农民、工人还是科技公司的亿万富翁,耕种、烹饪和享用食物的艺术都与身为中国人的意义深刻交织在一起。在中国,"你吃过饭了吗?"是朋友和邻居间互相问候的方式。食物是生意、快乐、健康和幸福。食物就是人生。它是将所有中国人联结在一起的粘合剂,无论他们的背景、社交圈或银行存款余额如何。

美食之旅

中国幅员辽阔,包括雄伟壮阔的山脉和河流、热带雨林、草原、沙漠和海岸。当太阳在长城的最东边落下时,还需要将近两个小时才能在沿着古老的丝绸之路进入中亚的长城最西端看到日落。当戴着草帽的稻农在贵州等南方地区播种时,在数千公里以北的天寒地冻的黑龙江,穿着毛皮大衣的渔民正在冰上凿洞捕捞。

中国拥有令人难以置信的气候和地形多样性,几千年来中华文明在此繁衍生息,意味着几乎无穷无尽的美食和佳肴。南下广东,你会尝到传统的早餐点心,餐车上堆满了烧麦、饺子、"凤爪"(又名鸡爪)、甜蛋挞和其他精致小菜,佐以杯杯茶饮,让人大快朵颐。

在中国的四川盆地,从面条到豆腐再到牛蛙,每样东西都配上一两味"麻辣"——辣椒与令人嘴巴发麻的四川花椒的结合。在青岛沿海,人们一边喝着著名的青岛啤酒,一边用成堆的炒蛤蜊下酒。在干旱的甘肃,回族穆斯林厨师将筋道的麦面团反复拉成丝,然后下到牛肉汤里。在南部边陲,毗邻老挝、越南和缅甸的云南,你餐餐都能嗦食美味的米线,而不用担心发出的声音惹人不快。

庆典美食

在中国,大餐是一种生活方式,餐桌往往是人生中许多里程碑和难忘时刻背景。每年农历新年,这里都会有全世界规模最大的人口迁移,千百万人回家与亲人一起庆祝农历新年。对于许多工薪家庭来说,平日里亲人们像种子一样散落在全国各地,唯有春节是他们一年一度团聚的日子,所以除夕夜的"团圆饭"成了一年中最珍贵隆重的一餐。盛宴通常以丰盛的吉祥菜肴为主菜,比如鱼类,听起来像是富余的"余";还有全家人一起参与的包饺子,它们外形与古代银锭相似,寓意是财富和好运。

一年中的大多数时候,中国人就餐都是家庭式的,用餐者共享菜肴而不分餐。这种就餐的方式象征着亲密与团结,即使只有少数朋友、同学或同事在一起吃饭。在互动式美食体验中最能感受到共享式用餐的乐趣,例如火锅,用餐者将生肉、蔬菜、豆腐等食材放入烧开冒泡的汤锅中,自行烹制食物。火锅口味有非常辣的,比如著名的重庆火锅辣到人大汗淋漓；也有口味相对清淡的，比如北京风味的涮羊肉，把手切羊肉片放入清汤中煮熟，然后蘸上芝麻酱再食用。

美食历史

许多著名的中国菜都与过去有着深远的联系。在 14 世纪，北京烤鸭是御膳，帝王的菜肴。后来这个食谱很可能流入了富家宅院和餐馆。其中一些成为日后家喻户晓的老字号品牌。今日在京城随处可见的烤鸭老字号"便宜坊"创建于 1416 年；4 个世纪后成立的另一个老字号"全聚德"，则开创了挂炉烤鸭的新手法，用果木为燃料，把鸭子挂在明炉中烹饪，把果木的芳香烤入鸭肉中，然后用薄面饼裹起来食用。

历史上，饮食也一直与中医和健康息息相关。唐朝（618—907）出现了许多关于饮食之道的文献，涵盖饮食、营养和食疗。时至今日，中国人依然相信胃是通向整体健康和幸福的道路。

美食纷呈

因为中餐大多使用筷子为餐具，以及常用酱油等调味品，所以其他国家往往误认为中餐有同质化的特点。事实上，中国遍布着面积相近、口味多样、工艺多样的美食区，这一点与欧洲国家相近。在干燥寒冷的北方小麦带，紧实的面包、筋道的面条和饺子以及炖肉和腌制食品占据了大部分食谱。而北方对酸奶的热爱则来自于以前长城外草原牧区的蒙古族人和满族人。在喜马拉雅高原的最西端，藏菜以糌粑（一种用大麦粉烤制的主食）和富含牦牛油的奶茶为主。

相比之下，中国南方水源充足的地区则以水稻、丰富的农产品和海鲜为主要食物，那里的人们对新鲜食材和完美烹饪非常痴迷。长江下游的淮扬菜，与苏州园林一样艺术、精巧。在曾经算得上偏远的云南地区，有 20 多个独具特色的少数民族，当地人的食物从可食用的花卉到稀有的山野蘑菇应有尽有；甚至还有炸山羊奶酪。历史上，中国菜被细分为"八大菜系"，但实际上，地区差异还可以进一步细分。每个地方——甚至是小镇——都以某些食物而闻名，像是核桃或是西瓜。有些地方则有自己的招牌菜，比如上海的汤包，或者中国瓷都景德镇的"景德鸡"。

食为天

中国有句俗语："民以食为天。"尽管这句话源自大约 2000 年前汉代的一篇古文，但今天它比以往任何时候都更加真实可信。过去半个世纪中国的变化速度令人慨叹，但不变的是中国与食物的文化关联。与过去相比，尽管如今的中国城市可能看起来已经完全不同，但在农产品、产地和菜肴形式这些方面，中华食物古老的特征依然生生不息。在瞬息万变的中国，食物是文化认同感最重要的支柱之一。对食物的热爱、欣赏和理解定义了一个中国人的特质，无论未来发生什么，这一点都不会改变。如今，在全球各地都能享用到中餐，但若要真正理解中餐的文化内涵，感受其种类的万千变化，还是只有在中国亲自品鉴才行。

Unit 5

Text A

了解你的老师

"你的浏览器记录别删了啊!"林凯(音译)提醒他11岁的儿子。而他的儿子正在上着学校老师讲的网课。林先生是有理由感到焦虑的,为了抑制疫情传播,政府要求学校无限期延迟开学。不过,教育部表示"停课不停学"。通告之下,全国最大规模的远程学习活动,正在家长们的监督下进行。林先生家住东部城市杭州,有一次,他发现了儿子被网游分心了。林先生想让他儿子知道,他会检查浏览器来看看儿子有没有调皮。

还有其他方法能加强纪律。武汉理工大学的刘卫华(音译)老师,会在网课时冷不防的点名。刘卫华解释说,由于现在不可能进行线下考试,所以他的评分会更加注重于学生的课堂讨论表现。这都是在阿里巴巴的钉钉或腾讯的课堂上进行的。

岳裘(音译)是一名北京的高中教师,她表示,家里网速慢不是偷懒的借口。如果网络波动太大导致无法进行视频电话时,学生可以下载音频文件和作业;同时,还鼓励家长在旁边进行监督。北京市政府发布通告,双职工家庭,一人可带薪在家带孩子。

在贫困农村地区,一些家庭上不了网,电视教学则弥补了这一不足。自2月17号以来,中国教育电视台每个工作日早上8点至晚上10点就在播出相关课程。每天第一节课是针对小学一年级学生的,适合年级更高学生的课程会在下午和晚上播出。所有的核心科目,如数学和语文,都包含在内。

高三学生最能感受到疫情对他们的影响了,因为即将迎接他们的就是高考。许多家长担心在线学习质量远比不上课堂教学。今年夏天,侯凯旋(音译)将在北部城市张家口参加高考,他热切地盼着学校重新开学。他说:"我就是在实体课堂里更有效率。"

不过,也不是他所有的同学都这样认为的。凯旋认为他一部分同学在家和在学校一样用功,并且那些同学还会为其他人肯定会有所懈怠而感到窃窃自喜。(值得庆幸的是,高三已经没啥新知识学了,重点在于复习。)

岳老师预测,到学校重新开学时,课堂就可能不一样了,师生关系更能会不那么"等级森严"了。原因是中国在线学习这一试验的延长减少了师生间的那份保留。以前不愿在微信上透露联系方式的老师,现在要依靠微信来回答学生的提问。在岳老师的学校,学生们甚至会打电话给老师,寻求反馈。如果他的预测是对的,那么这种壁垒被打破可能是疫情流行衍生出来为数不多令人开心的事。

Text B

所有国家都要用上海的数学教育方法吗？

中国上海于2009年和2012年参加了三年一届的国际学生评价项目（PISA）比赛，参赛选手都是15岁的中学生，他们在数学水平测验荣获第一名，远超德国、英国、美国，甚至新加坡和日本等国家。原因何在呢？

上海小学教师的教学生涯与大多数其他国家教师的教学生涯大不相同。比如，上海所有的老师都专攻一个科目——教数学的老师只教数学。

这些专业学科的教师要接受至少五年的培训，该培训针对特定年龄的学生，培训期间他们会对自己所教授的科目和学生的学习方式有更深入的理解。

培训合格后，小学教师通常每天只上两节课，其余时间用来帮助学生解决学习以外的问题以及与同事讨论教学技巧。

伦敦阿什伯纳姆社区学校的校长本·麦克马伦说："相比之下，如果现在的小学英语教师是直接接受所在学校的培训，那么他们可能只需在第一年的教师培训年份里接受五天的培训。培训后的第一年或第二年可能还有一些跟进式培训，如嵌入式培训和工作人员会议等。但这些只接受了寥寥数天培训的教师，与接受了针对特定科目的五年专业培训的专家级教师完全没有可比性。"

上海的中学也是相似的情况，老师们上课的时间较少，更多时间在帮学生做规划，帮助他们提升自己。

还有一些其他的区别：上海的学校上课时间更长：从早上7点到下午4点或5点；班级人数更多；课堂时间更短：每节课35分钟，接着是15分钟的非结构化活动时间。

英国教育部每年会派一些教师团队去上海参观和学习，麦克马伦就是其中一个团队的一员。他说，上海的中小学不会按能力分班，每个学生都理解后，老师才会继续讲课。因此，刚学习算术的时候，上海学生的基本算术教学比英国慢得多。

他说："上海的老师看了我们的课程，感到非常震惊，觉得我们想教的东西太多了。"

"他们到四年级或者五年级的时候才会教分数。因为他们觉得到那时，学生们才能熟练运用乘除法。"

"这本质上是一个'掌握式教学法'：教学内容少，进度慢，确保班上的每个学生共同前进，老师一遍又一遍地讲解知识点，直到学生们真正理解。"

看来，中国大陆其他城市的数学水平可能与上海相差甚远。因为在2015年的PISA比赛中，上海与北京、江苏和广东组成的团队在数学水平测验中落后于新加坡、日本、中国台湾和中国香港，排名第五。

有人认为，2015年上海没能取得第一可能是由于有大约四分之一的城市学生参加

了比赛。但PISA坚持认为，比赛结果表明上海工人家庭的孩子比西方专业人士家的孩子表现更佳。

伦敦大学学院全球繁荣研究所的成员亨利埃塔·摩尔说，这种教学系统的一个主要闪光点就是：它帮助挖掘贫困儿童的潜力，增加了社会流动性。不过，该系统也有缺陷。

摩尔说："在'努力了就有回报'这一观念的驱动下，你不会去想自己存在什么欠缺之处——因此，中国的数学老师目前正努力解决的一个问题就是创造力问题——解决这个问题需要时间仔细斟酌。"

"实际上，我们英国在创造力方面做得更好。中国也正在努力改善，并向我们学习。"

还有人批评在这个教学系统下，父母给了孩子们太过繁重的学习任务。据估计，80%的中国学生都在上校外辅导班。

摩尔说："父母过度关注孩子的教育有一个缺点：他们变得非常要强——比自己的孩子还要强——所以他们恨不得让孩子上所有的辅导班。"

那么，如果其他国家采用这个系统，效果如何？

牛津大学的数学荣休教授安妮·沃森说："我会采用这样的想法，即任何一个教数学的人都需要深入了解数学的概念结构和学生的学习方法。我也会接受对每个人都有高期望的想法。"

网络创业者玛莎·莱恩·福克斯对此表示赞同。

她说："这个想法——与我认为的情形不同，英国的每个人至少都可以成为数学大师——有两个地方很吸引我：一是我很喜欢对微小的细节给予的这种令人难以置信的关注；二是我对这种渐进式和小模块化的教学概念真的很感兴趣。"

"这种教学策略基于正确的原则，它鼓励人们相信数学可以挖掘每个人的潜力。"

麦克马伦说，他管理的小学已经借鉴了上海学校的一些想法。

不按能力分班，增加学生之间的互动，因此，课堂上出现了一种"不一样的气氛"。

麦克马伦说："学校里表现优异的低年级学生有很强的数学、计算和概念意识。"

他还说，对于教师而言，还有另外一个好处：不会抹杀学生们的创造力。

Unit 6

Text A

儒家思想下矛盾的中国人

连续20天在微博（中国版Twitter）上成为十大热门话题之一绝非易事。3月1日在省级电视台首映的一部电视剧《都挺好》就做到了。这部电视剧讲述了一个虚构的中国家庭被内部矛盾所冲击的故事。女主角苏明玉几乎和她丧偶的父亲和二哥不通往来。这位父亲是个爱唠叨的怪人，他希望他的两个成年儿子为他的奢侈喜好买单。而这导致了兄弟之间不断的争吵，他们都不想被冠上不孝顺的名号。

《都挺好》累计播放量已超过3.9亿次。这比收视率排名第二的电视剧高2.78亿次。从《辛普森一家》到《权力的游戏》，关于家庭矛盾的电视剧在许多国家很常见。《都挺好》中对盲目顺从的传统价值观的质疑引起了轰动。令观众震惊的是它对中产阶级毫无掩盖的罕见写照。

许多中国人都能理解苏家的困境。女儿对父亲怀恨在心，尤其是对已故的母亲恨之入骨，因为父母虐待自己，却纵容两位哥哥。当她还是孩子的时候就被要求洗哥哥的衣服。二哥打她的时候父母视而不见。中国从1979年开始实行计划生育政策，2016年改为二孩政策。电视剧中的场景勾起了许多1979年之前出生的女性痛苦的回忆。一些人在社交媒体上分享了家庭性别歧视的故事。

但最引起热议的是该剧对孝道的批判。即使在今天，对父母忠贞不渝的儒家思想仍然是备受尊崇的。许多人认为，衡量一个人是否坚守这一美德最好的方法就是看他能否在父母年迈时照顾好他们。今日头条（一款中国新闻应用）最近开展的一项调查显示，中国有54%的老年人一半以上的支出由其成年子女们承担。毫无疑问，这在一定程度上是由于养老金体系不够完善所致。但来自北京的一位《都挺好》的粉丝表示，这也反映了一种"永远不要对父母说不"的文化。

然而在剧中，这位丧偶的父亲并没有引起人们太多的同情。他大发脾气，并坚持让大儿子给他买一套三居室的公寓（虽然儿子很不情愿地买了）。社交媒体上的评论者们已经把这位父亲称为"巨婴"——他们说这是现实生活中的父母们所拥有的一个共同的特征。苏家的孩子们尽到他们的责任了，但观众们还是应该为他们所表达的不满而鼓掌。

官方媒体对该剧的评论褒贬不一。一家报纸写道，"贴近现实的情节和表演"触及了许多观众的"痛点"。然而，《北京日报》则称该剧是"不切实际的"。它写道，该剧"不合理"地把老年人"可能拥有的每一种坏毛病"集于一人之身，以此来讽刺年迈的父母。

Text B

一孩还是两孩？这是个问题

北京——尽管20世纪70年代开始启用、2016年初被废弃的独生子女政策一直被视作中国最严格的法律之一，但它达到了预期的效果——控制中国人口增长。

三十多年来，随着经济繁荣和自然的发展，国家面临着一个新的人口问题：看起来，中国将在变富之前先变老。

37岁的史华欣喜若狂，他的第二个女儿上月出生，但是关于二胎将影响他家的年度花销这件事，他就显得没那么开心了。他估计，这个新生儿每年的花销大约为两万元（2891美元）。

史说："钱还不是我们最大的顾虑。我们担心能否确保把我们的孩子送进最好的学校。"

史说："有两个孩子意味着谁也不会孤单地长大，但是即便政府允许，我也不想再要了。两个足够了。"

继2013年的政策缓和允许父母中一方是独生子女的夫妇生二胎后，2016年1月1日起，所有结婚夫妇允许有两个孩子。

尽管采取了以上政策，并对少数民族和农村夫妇提供了补贴，中国正在面临劳动力短缺的问题。据计划生育协会统计，2015年中国处于工作年龄的人口只有10亿多，但是，这一数据将在2030年下降到9.58亿，2050年下降到8.27亿。

计划生育协会副会长王培安说，政府关注到了人口的变化，意识到调整计划生育政策刻不容缓。

"不敢生"

一儿一女组成了汉字"好"，寓意不错。尽管定居在天津的34岁的郑娟想要一个二胎组成"好"，但她既没欲望也没有获得支持来扩充家庭。

她说："自从我的女儿2011年出生以来，我的父母一直照顾她，因为我的丈夫和我都在工作。他们年纪太大，没法再照顾一个孩子，我们没钱雇个好保姆。"

和史华一样，郑娟也关注教育。为了保证她家位于优质小学学区，去年她在办公室附近买了一套250万元的公寓，这样她就能在学校、公司两头跑了。

根据全国妇联的调查，在10个省级地区1万个拥有15岁以下儿童的家庭中，53.3%的人表示没有要二胎的欲望。

大多数父母考虑二胎时的主要因素就是学校质量、婴儿用品、生活环境和医疗设施。如果家庭能够负担得起第二个孩子，其他主要的顾虑包括晚孕对母亲是否安全，以及学前儿童保育。

妇联儿童部主任陈小霞说，单就经济顾虑而言，就意味着很多家庭不敢或不想要二胎。

陈说："有二孩的家庭有新的需求。他们需要建议和指导。"

现在需要更多的支持

据妇联数据，2016年上半年，中国拥有831万新生儿，比之前一年上涨6.9%。在这些新生儿中，44.6%是二胎，比例上涨6.7%。

自2015年12月以来，约3万名妇女在北京登记怀孕，然而北京只有大约4900张产妇床位，只能服务25000名产妇。

据中国协和医科大学出版社 2015 年卫生统计年鉴，中国每 1000 个儿童仅对应 0.43 名儿科医生。

据国家健康和计划生育委员会统计，计划生育政策的放松，意味着截至 2020 年中国需要增添 8.9 万张产妇床位，14 万多名产妇医生。

不同省份已经采取行动支持想要二胎的女性，计划为她们提供更长时间的带薪产假。

在发达国家，女性或有同等或接近男性教育水平和工资水平的机会。年轻人的生活方式——他们对于结婚或生孩子的兴趣——彻底改变，导致许多女性推迟生育，直到 30 多岁才要小孩。

2016 年 11 月下旬，中国社会科学院发布了《中国人口与劳动报告》，显示二孩政策并不是计划生育改革的"终点"。

为了避免"低出生率陷阱"，中国将继续观察其人口数据，一旦需要进一步放宽计划生育政策，将采取措施进行干预。最近的计划生育政策改革，如果说有什么区别的话，那就是标志着一个新时代的诞生。

Unit 7

Text A

淡茶不易卖
——一位美籍华人电影明星解释了为什么国际巨制在中国遭遇惨败

即便超级英雄电影《复仇者联盟：终局之战》中没有"美国队长"这个角色，它也是一部非常引人注目的美国大片。作为《复仇者联盟》系列电影的最后一部，它除了华丽和昂贵的特效外，还凸显了各有缺陷、个人主义的超级英雄。在中国，这部电影刚刚打破首映周末票房纪录，这一现象可能会让外界猜测中美电影市场——即世界上最大的两个电影市场——正在趋于同化。而事实上，中国电影正变得越来越独特和自信。

多年来，好莱坞制片人们斥巨资打造了一系列影片，并认为美国观众和中国观众没有太大不同，都会为同一部精心打造的全球化电影欢笑、哭泣和欢呼。然而，中国电影市场总是证明他们错了。《复仇者联盟》系列电影在中国拥有庞大而独特的粉丝群体，他们总说喜欢这系列电影的缘由正是因为他们认同与所处环境格格不入的英雄们，在一个残酷、批判的世界中挣扎前行。

去年中国电影票房超过 17 亿元，创下国内纪录。大部分票房增长都是由国产大片推动的，其中包括描述中国海外军事英雄事迹的《红海行动》，以及一部关于癌症主题、悲喜交加的《我不是药神》。尽管好莱坞在 2018 年的全球票房表现不俗，进口电影在中国的营收却在逐年下降。

在《复仇者联盟：终局之战》上映之前，本年度全球最成功的电影是中国科幻史诗电影《流浪地球》。但这主要归功于这部电影在自己国家的受欢迎程度。截至该片在美国下映，该片在美国的票房收入还不到总票房收入的 1%。西方影评人很难把该片和拯救地球联系起来，因为这部电影中唯一非中国人的角色由俄罗斯人扮演。

中美混血演员卢靖姗以专业的角度谈到这两个电影市场。卢靖姗曾在香港就读中小学，大学就读于伦敦政治经济学院，她精通粤语、英语和普通话。她曾在电影《战狼 2》中饰演女主角，该片于 2017 年上映，是迄今为止票房收入最高的中国电影。

这是一部发人深省的成功之作：该片以饱受战争蹂躏的非洲为背景，讲述了一名中国突击队员从邪恶的美国雇佣兵手中营救中国和非洲人质的故事。

卢靖姗从洛杉矶出差回到北京，准备去挪威参加电视节目，本栏目（茶馆专栏）在这间隙采访了她。她表示：两年前，好莱坞制片人正在设法制作既能在美国又能在中国大卖的影片。这可能要在美国大片中加入一位中国女演员扮演"装饰性角色"。如今卢靖姗在美国参加的会见都"与中国因素有关"。她指的是使用美国技术、但直接面向中国观众的合拍片。

如果好莱坞放弃那些旨在吸引所有文化的项目，并且不冒犯任何文化，这位女演员就不会如此哀叹。她将这类电影的审批过程比作把同一个茶包泡在 10 个杯子里，然后从最后一个杯子里喝下去。在中国方面，她看到中国电影公司对海外市场兴趣不足："若中国电影市场需求如此之大，为何还要迎合全球市场的口味呢？"

海外热门电影在中国票房不佳，她对此并不感到意外。尽管卢靖姗的美国形象与《摘金奇缘》有关，但她表示，她的中国形象过于夸张，甚至"异想天开"。她说，中国观众喜欢看到浪漫的英雄以微妙的方式表达爱；"可能是他给她夹菜的方式。"

国家规划正发挥作用。咨询公司 IHS Markit 表示，中国去年新开了 9303 家影院。政府的目标是到 2020 年在全国范围内投放 8 万个屏幕，如今已有 6 万个。一些公司将在片源供应过剩和优质影片短缺的情况下苦苦挣扎。但是，电影的扩张提升了中国小城市电影市场的影响力，因为小城市的观众更喜欢本土题材的电影。

Text B

《星球大战》在中国为何屡战屡败？

攻势如虹：500 名帝国冲锋队员占领了长城；X 翼战机穿梭在上海和北京城中；光剑噼啪作响，交错在全国各地的影院里。

而数百万中国观影者的反应是：又是这些？谁爱看谁看去。

《星球大战》是历史上最成功的系列电影之一，然而尽管努力打入中国市场，它在中国这个为其他电影中的英雄、怪兽和机器人贡献了大量票房的市场接连受挫。最新的《星球大战》电影《天行者崛起》仍未摆脱这一趋势：该片在全球范围内获得了近10亿美元的票房，在华票房仅勉强突破2000万美元。

之前几部《星球大战》系列电影也好不到哪里去，其原因包括历史、地缘政治，以及中国观众明显缺乏美国观众的那种怀旧情绪。2015年，《原力觉醒》在美国的首映票房接近2.5亿美元；两年后，《最后的绝地武士》也取得了同样的成绩；《天行者崛起》上月上映的头几天就获得了1.77亿美元的票房。

在中国，这些影片的首映票房分别为5200万美元、2800万美元和1200万美元。

管理中国最大星战迷网站"星球大战中文网"的陈涛（音译）估计，中国影迷俱乐部的会员总数不足200人。

几年前，随着《最后的绝地武士》在中国的票房下滑，北京大学生徐梦（音译）在接受《南华早报》采访时说，电影制片人应该尝试采用新故事、新角色——以及一个全新的名字。她说："新的《星球大战》续集不冠以《星球大战》这个名字会好一点。"

另一名学生郎逸飞（音译）称星战系列电影"沉重且阴郁"，并表示，"我认为他们应该放弃老故事。"

尽管迪士尼积极地努力推广《星球大战》，但该系列在中国的收益仍在不断减少。公司用上了迷你帝国冲锋队员和实物大小的星际战机，并与中国合作伙伴在一系列项目上展开合作，包括翻译相关书籍，制作一个中韩男子组合的音乐视频。

这样的行为突显出在中国电影市场赚钱有多么重要。中国目前已是全球第二大电影市场。最新的《复仇者联盟》系列电影在中国的票房收入超过5亿美元，《变形金刚》和《速度与激情》等系列电影的票房收入持续达到数亿美元。

电影历史学家和业内专家表示，造成这些好莱坞大片之间的收入差距的原因在于《速度与激情：特别行动》和《侏罗纪世界》这样的续集基本上可以独立于前作而存在，而且中国观众是伴随着漫威（Marvel）漫画英雄等系列影片长大的，不是看着最早的《星球大战》长大的。

"这样一来整个系列的前六部基本上就被抹去了，"加州大学洛杉矶分校中国文学与电影教授白睿文（Michael Berry）说，"没机会让人对星战着迷。"

佛罗里达大学中国研究与电影教授肖莹说："这部电影有些深奥、复杂的术语和情节，对于没有看过整个系列的中国观众来说，很难理解、消化和欣赏其魅力。"

虽然前三部电影带来了无数周边商品，在上映期结束后人们依然保持着对影片的兴趣，但在中国，除了一些照搬《星球大战》中的形象、却与电影本身无关的连环画，这些电影基本上还是默默无闻。

家长不会把自己的《星球大战》玩偶、午餐盒或录像带传给孩子。在世纪之交，随着中国影院的开放，《星球大战》前传三部曲在中国上映，那个时候，"天行者"还是一个陌生的词。

肖莹还指出，近些日子里，国产片已经占据了中国电影票房的大头。其中包括最新的武打片《叶问4》和《流浪地球》，后者是"硬"科幻小说比"科幻肥皂剧"《星球大战》更受中国观众欢迎的实例。

娱乐公司家赋（Jiaflix）总裁马克·加尼斯（Marc Ganis）说，在过去十年里，中国的电影产业在制作、导演、营销和表演方面已经成熟。他指出,《星球大战》在日本、韩国等其他亚洲国家遭遇了来自本国电影更加激烈的竞争。

对于《星球大战》的衍生电影《星球大战外传：侠盗一号》，迪士尼选用了亚洲观众熟知的两位明星——甄子丹和姜文，但收效甚微。

在2018年的一次采访中，甄子丹将该片在中国的失败归因于其漫长的背景故事，他把它与漫画改编电影的相对简单以及取得的成功进行了比较。"漫威电影理解起来要容易得多，"他说，"而《星球大战》里有整个宇宙。"

仿佛就是为了佐证他的观点，《复仇者联盟4：终局之战》2019年在中国上映首周末的票房，超过了所有《星球大战》首映票房之和。

弗吉尼亚大学教授、《中国制造好莱坞》一书的作者孔安怡（Aynne Kokas）说，正传三部曲的一些卖点——比如在70年代和80年代令观众叹为观止的特效——到了21世纪仅仅是讨人喜欢的雕虫小技，而远非革命性的划时代创举。

她说："在西方,《星球大战》可谓一种时代印记，是一种可以与子女分享经历的体验。"她还指出，该系列的内容主要是关于家庭，充满回忆、不断演变的神话和时代变迁。

她表示："我们已经看到了很多衍生品，很多的衍生人物，极力重现正传三部曲的魔力。而在中国，这没能吸引观众"。

孔安怡说，电视连续剧《曼达洛人》中的角色尤达宝宝是星战系列试图重现其经典之作的例子。"现在没有了尤达，我们正在努力将《星球大战》的魔力带入下一代。"

Unit 8

Text A

中国网红：Papi酱，语速飞快的邻家女孩

北京——姜逸磊是一个在凌乱的公寓客厅里念叨减肥问题和唠叨父母的邻家女孩。她留着刘海，化着淡妆，还养了两只猫。

她也是中国蹿红速度最快、知名度最高的网络名人之一，人称Papi酱。她的商业合作伙伴说，在不到一年的时间里，她用自己语速飞快的碎碎念视频在多个平台吸引了4400万粉丝。

尽管粉丝数量在各个平台上可能会有一些重叠，但这个数字已经超越了瑞安·比

嘉（Ryan Higa，1780万）和詹娜·马布尔（Jenna Marbles，1640万）等YouTube名人的粉丝数量。

上个月，姜逸磊的直播首秀（一段时长90分钟，随便聊聊毫无剧本的视频）在一天内就获得7400万次观看。这比泰勒·斯威夫特（Taylor Swift）的最新音乐视频《新浪漫主义》(New Romantics) 在YouTube上用四个月获得的观看次数还要多。

毫无疑问，许多事物在中国的规模都会比在世界其他地方大。但即便以在中国的标准来衡量，29岁的姜逸磊也算得上出类拔萃，以至于中国媒体机构开始称她为"2016年头号网络红人"。

Papi酱是迄今为止最受追捧的网络名人，"总部位于北京的网上社区应用玲珑沙龙的首席执行官于困困说，"中国很多年轻人都视Papi酱为偶像。"

姜逸磊的迅速走红，反映了中国互联网快速变化的本质，尤其是中国网民对内容的激增需求。

具有官方背景的中国互联网信息中心于本月发布的一份报告显示，中国的网络已经越来越多地由移动端驱动，在7.1亿中国网民中，有超过92%的人使用手机上网。他们在网上购物，交友聊天，在微博和微信等应用中获取资讯，进行娱乐。

这导致中国人口中的"自媒体"的数量不断增长。"自媒体"是一个涵盖性的术语，即自己在社交媒体平台上发布内容用户的统称。

姜逸磊之前在中央戏剧学院的同学、如今的商业合伙人杨铭在接受采访时表示，"我看到自媒体做得越来越大，就想'我们是不是也该试一试？'"（姜逸磊本人很少与媒体接触，拒绝了本刊的采访请求。）

杨铭表示，直到2015年年中，中国都还没有多少人做短视频。而在美国，YouTube名人几年前就出现了，已经不稀奇了。"当时还不叫短视频，"他说，"就是视频。"

姜逸磊之前在娱乐业工作了几年，做过舞台演员、副导演，之后返回中央戏剧学院读研。这个时候，她开始做一些尝试，运用一些充满创意的元素进行表演，例如经过数字处理的声音、飞快的语速和跳跃式的剪辑，而这些后来成为她标志性风格的一部分。慢慢地，她的粉丝数量逐渐增长。直到2015年11月的一天，她做的一部拿上海女人说话"夹生饭"（中文夹杂英文的说话方式）习惯开涮的短视频在网上疯狂流传。

"当时我就愣住了，吓得半死，"她在今年6月接受新浪网采访时说。"这可怎么办啊，饭都吃不下了。"

自打那时起，她的视频聚焦于受过教育的都市年轻人颇为熟悉的话题——比如劈腿的男友、明星文化和方言——总共制作了60多个视频。在一个令人印象深刻的视频中，她充分而又直率地表达了自己有多厌恶人们一谈恋爱就把恋爱对象挂在嘴上。在另一个视频中，她探讨了中国人关于性别的刻板印象。

"我们在平常生活中经常会听到这样一些话，"她对着镜头说道。"这个工作太累了，不适合女性。"剪辑。"姑娘家家的打什么篮球啊。"剪辑。"女人还是要长头发才像个女人。"剪辑。"女人搞搞同性恋就算了，男的我可真受不了。"剪辑。"男护士？矮油。"（译者注：矮油是网络流行语，即以夸张的语气说'哎呦'）

这段两分钟长的视频以"我是Papi酱，一个集美貌与才华于一身的女子"作结。这句话已经成了她的口头禅。

姜逸磊的粉丝以沿海城市二三十岁的年轻人为主，出生于上海的姜逸磊为他们提供了中国喜剧中难得一见的生动城市视角。

"以前有赵本山之类的喜剧演员，但那常常是一种极为乡野的幽默，讲的笑话都和耕地、吃韭菜之类的事情有关，"玲珑沙龙CEO于困困说。

她还说："另一方面，Papi酱很受白领人士喜爱，他们想要讨论的是自己怎么39岁了还没结婚，该怎么办。"

随着她的一夜爆红，姜逸磊逐渐受到互联网企业和投资者的关注。近年来，由于有关部门打击盗版内容，企业对国内本土原创内容的渴求十分强烈。

在此背景下，能自己写、拍、剪的姜逸磊显然有其吸引力。

今年3月，姜逸磊成为中国网络名人当中首批吸引到资本投资的人。由四家大机构投资商组成的团体宣布，向她的公司注资1200万元。

其中一名投资人罗振宇在接受澎湃采访时谈到了Papi酱："在现在网红一代一代更替的市场形态中，我们认为Papi酱能够改变市场，并注入全新的商业逻辑。"罗振宇本人创办并主持了一档热门在线脱口秀。

拿到这笔投资后，姜逸磊及其商业合伙人如今在专心创办并运营PapiTube平台。他们开始在这一平台上支持与捧红其他的年轻自媒体人。

不过，他们可能面临一些困难。今年4月，中国在广播电视领域的最高监管机构要求姜逸磊净化视频中不时出现的不当用语，迫使她暂时撤下了多数视频。这被广泛视为官方发出的一个信号：要对网络名人加强管控。

不过，她的吸引力似乎并未受到影响。被审查机构斥责的事情发生了仅仅几天后，她以2200万元的价格将一条视频贴片广告拍卖给了上海的一家在线化妆品零售商。（她表示计划将这笔钱捐给中央戏剧学院。）

重中之重，现在最大的问题是，姜逸磊能否持续产出高质量的内容。尽管她每周发布新视频，可她好像还在适应自己的红人地位。

在新浪6月的采访中，当被问到她为何没在拍卖当天露面时，她只回答了一个词："紧张。"

Text B

隐居一隅的美食博主，疫情期间的田园女王——李子柒

和许多疫情期间的居家厨师一样，我会在葱的绿色部分吃完后，把长着根须的葱白放进一杯水里重新生长，并为自己的朴素俭省而欢欣雀跃。

但上周，中国网络红人李子柒在 YouTube 上发布了一段名为《蒜的一生》(*The Life of Garlic*) 的烹饪视频后，我真希望自己能早点从窗台上种葱这个阶段毕业。

在这段长达 12 分钟、浏览量超过 700 万次的视频中，李子柒把蒜瓣种进她家外面的一块土地上。时间流逝，蒜苗生长，伸向天空。

李子柒用新鲜的青蒜苗炒猪肉。收获蒜头之后，她把茎秆编成辫子，挂起来晾干，剩下的用来腌渍和保存，用其中一些给鸡爪和拌菜调味。

李子柒住在四川省的一个小村庄里，很少接受媒体采访。她梳着皇冠辫子，身穿银色毛皮斗篷，在雪地里优雅行走，看上去就像迪士尼的公主。29 岁的她因为在微博和 YouTube 上发布自给自足的农村生活的迷人视频而出名。

对于世界各地隔离中的观众来说，她这种一切自己动手的田园幻想，已经成为逃避和安慰的可靠来源。

我通常只打算看一个视频——就看一个——但之后就放任算法指引我再看一个，然后再看一个，直到在鸟鸣和乐曲的抚慰下，确信自己从她那里学到了不少如何靠土地为生的有用信息。

如果我曾经对着两打红薯不知所措，现在我已经知道应该如何用它们来提取淀粉并且做粉条了。我对自己这么说。就算一个人在荷塘里，我也知道该怎么采获和收拾莲藕。

李子柒的视频里不做任何解释。事实上，她喜欢安静地工作，不使用任何现代厨房设备。她的筛子是葫芦做的。她的刨丝器是一块金属片，自己穿了一些斜孔，固定在两块木头上。小溪就是她的盆子，她在那里清洗蔬菜上的污垢。

她的厨房跟我在洛杉矶的厨房完全不一样。但是一边用笔记本电脑看李子柒，一边吃着奶油爆米花当晚餐，我想我或许也可以像她那样快乐地生活，沉浸在乡村纯粹的自然之美当中，忠诚地使用极为传统的烹饪方式。

李子柒酿造桃花酒和樱桃酒，保存枇杷和玫瑰花瓣。她制作新鲜豆腐和汤汁清澈的兰州拉面，还从零开始发酵四川豆瓣酱。她宰杀鸭子和整只的动物。

她的出名不是靠急功近利。在一段关于松茸的视频里，她先是搭起烤松茸的烤架，一块一块地把砖头垒起来，刮平灰浆，然后在树林里搜寻蘑菇。

在一段关于焖鱼的视频里，她先是去钓鱼，在雪中耐心地把太小的鱼扔回去，雪花在她的头发里冻结。

就像某些末世后小说中的主人公一样，李子柒几乎总是一个人，不过她似乎并不孤独，她骑马穿过野花丛中，或者提着一篮一篮的红薯站在橘花树下。她似乎不知疲倦，专注，自信，独立。

这些视频让人深感慰藉。但是不仅如此——它们揭示了每道菜所有组成部分中倾注的复杂而密集的劳动，同时也让漫长而孤独的生产过程显得有意义和有价值。

这与大多数烹饪内容完全相反，那些内容暗示着一切都是那么简单快速，你也可以做到，而且可能用不了 30 分钟。

但是李子柒也浪漫化了农村生活的挣扎，而且像任何精明的网红一样，她也将这种魅力变现。她的网店里出售一种弯刀，类似于她在视频中使用的那种，还有以汉服为灵感设计的宽松亚麻服装、四川参蜜和辣椒酱。

按照李子柒自己的说法，她的故事是这样的：她十几岁时离家去找工作，后来又回到农村照顾祖母，然后开始记录自己的生活。虽然以前都是一个人拍视频，但现在她有了一个助手和一名摄像师。

"我只想让城里的人知道，他们吃的食物是从哪里来的，"去年秋天，李子柒在罕见地接受 Goldthread 采访时说。（她始终没有回应我的采访请求。）

但是，不管在中国还是美国，世界上的大部分食物都不是来自任何人的后院，也不是从零开始制作的。面条是在工厂里生产和包装的。鸡和猪在快速、危险的流水线上被宰杀。

工业供应链的脆弱性，以及在商业工厂和屠宰场工作的人们所面临的巨大风险，在过去几周中都暴露无遗。

李子柒完全回避了这个残缺体系的存在。这是她的视频在当下提供的最有力的幻想——人们自己种植和烹饪食物，不浪费任何东西，不需要太多身外之物。

在隔离中，看着李子柒独自采摘玫瑰花瓣和成熟的番茄的视频，我不禁思忖，这一切的背景是过去还是未来？这些视频是关于我们已失去的集体食物知识的记录，还是对其复兴的理想化愿景？